Writing with Families

Writing with Families

By S. Arthur Kelly

Maupin House Publishing, Inc.

Writing with Families
©2006 by Shawn Arthur Kelly

Family Writing Project® and **Family Scribes**ˢᴹ are proprietary service marks used in association with the writing program described in the book, *Writing with Families*, and are owned by the author, Shawn Arthur Kelly. These terms are being made available to readers, teachers, and other third parties for use on a royalty-free basis; provided those making use of either term agree to closely adhere to the philosophies and approaches described in *Writing with Families*, and to register with the author (www.familywritingprojects.com). Any other use is strictly prohibited.

Book and cover design: Mickey Cuthbertson
Cover Photo: S. Arthur Kelly
For comments and more information on The Family Writing Project and Family Scribe Groups, you may email the publisher at info@maupinhouse.com or the author at arthur@familywritingprojects.com.

Library of Congress Cataloging-in-Publication Data

Kelly, S. Arthur (Shawn Arthur), 1961-
  Writing with families / by S. Arthur Kelly.
     p. cm.
  ISBN-13: 978-0-929895-66-6 (pbk.)
  ISBN-10: 0-929895-66-5 (pbk.)
  1. Family social work. 2. School social work. 3. Writing--Social aspects. 4. Group facilitation. 5. Education--Parent participation. 6. Community and school. I. Title.
  HV697.K45 2006
  362.82'3--dc22
                        2006016658

The Family Writing Project website, www.FamilyWritingProjects.com, is dedicated to publicizing the work of Family Scribe Groups around the country and disseminating information about Family Scribe Groups. The website, www.WritingWithFamilies.com, offers ideas and information that expand upon the content of this book.

Maupin House publishes professional resources for K-12 educators. Contact us for tailored, in-school training or to schedule an author for a workshop or conference. Visit www.maupinhouse.com for free lesson plan downloads.

🍎 **Maupin House**

Maupin House Publishing, Inc.
2416 NW 71 Place
Gainesville, FL 32653
www.maupinhouse.com

800-524-0634
352-373-5588
352-373-5546 (fax)
info@maupinhouse.com

10 9 8 7 6 5 4 3 2 1

Dedication

To my parents, Bill and Kay Kelly, my first and most important teachers. Also, to the families and students of John C. Fremont Middle School in Las Vegas, Nevada, from whom I draw inspiration to teach and write.

Table of Contents

Foreword

Parents as Partners in Student Writing: Enlarging the Community of Learners

*M*ore than thirty years ago, researcher Joyce Epstein began to advise us of the importance of involving concerned adults in their children's education. Many others recognized its inherent wisdom, and the majority of improvement efforts from then on made explicit reference to parental engagement. Soon after, accreditation processes, codified reform efforts, and even mandated governance structures began to incorporate some forms of parental involvement. Yet despite all this attention, there was a relative dearth of practical advice about why and how to involve parents.

One important lesson learned from the extensive record of trial and error in regards to parental involvement is that we generally speak of involved parents in one of three ways: as *boosters and advocates* we turn to for supports (financial and political); in *governance arrangements* wherein we involve them to set and monitor direction for a school or system; or as *partners for learning* who are engaged directly in their children's learning. The first of these is a longstanding, traditional role with which the system is most comfortable. The second is relatively newer, and more meaningful forms of engagement are becoming fairly widespread.

However, it is unquestionably the last that offers the greatest payoff in terms of students' learning, and it is the one which, when arranged effectively, ensures parental engagement in the other two roles. It is ironic, then, that it is in this area where we have the fewest proven means of engaging parents and the least useful guidance. This resource changes that as it makes an important contribution to our knowledge and our craft in terms of family involvement in students' learning. It tells us *how*, but more importantly, it teaches us *to what end*—in ways that equip us to figure out *how* in our own contexts and circumstances.

Involving parents in family writing can serve children's growth and development in many powerful ways. First, it can enlarge the audience for students' writing. To have parents recognize and value their children's work elevates its importance in students' eyes. Second, it makes parents aware of the performance standards being applied in the classroom and involves them in setting and maintaining high aspirations for their children. Third, it increases the sophistication of parents' views about educational growth and development. They learn about educational practice, equipping them to better support the work of teachers. Fourth, parents have a deeper understanding of the school's performance, especially in relation to their own child. It is a more honest and exacting form of public accounting because it is expressed in terms that are intuitively understandable to one of the most important "publics" served by the schools. Fifth, and perhaps most important, parents learn a lot about their children— what concerns them, what they think about, what they value— information that can greatly enhance the interaction between parent and child.

In this book, Arthur Kelly describes an effort to engage parents in all these ways by involving them in their children's writing lives, by asking them to serve as critical readers of their children's work, and by having them contribute to the writing conversation through their own work. He describes how the program was conceived, organized, and carried out. He also presents and analyzes parents' and students' responses to these new roles and relationships and suggests how a family writing group can be used as a valuable part of the educational process in our schools. In doing so, he validates how parents themselves grow through the experience and how families are strengthened by it.

Arthur Kelly describes a "partnership" among students, families, and teachers. It is a partnership in the truest sense of the word. However, nowhere does he explicitly offer a definition of partnership—one that would challenge the reader to fully appreciate all he and his colleagues have accomplished in this program. I will offer a definition that has guided me for years: A partnership is a relationship in which the members have 1) common goals, 2) shared values, 3) equal power, and 4) real work to do.

True partnerships come about when folks work together and share the power equally, seeking perhaps to influence but also willing to be influenced by their partners (and trusting that their influence can be beneficial). This sort of partnership with families is the only way to make them feel welcomed into the school's conversation about student writing. As long as they are participating in that conversation, there is the opportunity to influence and profitably be influenced by parents' thinking. It is possible for parents to be more effective partners in their children's education, but only if they are engaged in the process. Apply this definition to the work of Kelly and his colleagues. It will reveal the depth of the program described in this book, and it qualifies Kelly's work as a partnership with families in the best possible sense.

Dr. Paul G. LeMahieu
Director of Research and Evaluation, National Writing Project—
University of California-Berkeley and University of Hawai'i-Mānoa

Acknowledgements

I owe quite a large debt of gratitude to a number of people and organizations whose interest and support of my work have made Family Scribe Groups successful. From the start, it has taken a community of supportive individuals and organizations to ignite and sustain my dream of writing with families in Las Vegas and around the country.

First, I must thank those families with whom I have collaborated in the Fremont Family Writing Project. The dedication and excitement you bring to our Family Scribe Group is what inspires me to teach and write. I extend that same appreciation to all of the amazing teachers and Family Scribe Group facilitators I have known and worked with over the past few years. Together, we have discovered—or perhaps rediscovered—why the things we do as teachers matter.

Next, I want to express my respect and appreciation to Rosemary Holmes-Gull and Dennis Goode, both of the Southern Nevada Writing Project, for their belief in my work and their constant encouragements. I would not have written this book if they had not told me, again and again, that the Family Scribe experience had to be shared with a much broader audience than I was able to reach in Las Vegas. Similarly, I want to thank Marilyn McKinney and Saralyn Lasley, also of the Southern Nevada Writing Project, for their research into the impact of Family Scribe Groups on students and their families.

In the National Writing Project, author and editor Art Peterson encouraged me to do my first serious writing about the Family Writing Project and Family Scribes, writing that appeared in the summer 2004 issue of the National Writing Project's journal, *The Quarterly*, as the article "No More Fear and Loathing in Las Vegas." Some ideas from that article appear in slightly changed form in the introduction to this book's text. Paul LeMahieu, director of research, evaluation, and information systems for the National Writing Project, was a great help, both with assisting me in shaping my thinking about how Family Scribe Groups impact student learners, and with the Southern Nevada Writing Project's research into the successes of Family Scribe Groups. This support from Art and Paul at the national level encouraged me to press on with my research and writing.

Jocelyn Bluitt and Alma Estrada, from the City of Las Vegas Youth Neighborhood Association Partnership Program, have each shown tireless support of our project's gardens, murals, and citywide family writing fair. Thanks to you both for helping us to surpass our project's goals as a community partner. I also want to applaud the City of Las Vegas City Council, Councilman Gary Reese, and the Honorable Mayor Oscar Goodman for supporting our work with the families of John C. Fremont Middle School. This involvement by the City of Las Vegas validated our concern for our school's community and greatly motivated all of us to focus on our lives as Las Vegans in our writings and projects.

At John C. Fremont Middle School, I want to thank all the teachers and administrators who over the years have found ways to help our project. Special thanks go to the following: George Leavens, our former vice principal, who rolled up his sleeves to work in the garden alongside our families and students on many spring afternoons; Tierney Cushman, who consistently amazes with her thoughtfulness and assistance; Ben Montoya, our principal, who has always been encouraging and resourceful; and especially to my English department peers Kim Sicurella, Beverly Davison, and Melanie De La Cruz, each of whom have contributed ideas and energy that have kept the Fremont Family Writing Project moving along year after year.

I am thankful for the support of my wife, Magaly, for enduring my habit of secluding myself at the cabin for weeks at a time to sort out my thoughts and figure out how to get them to line up as words on the screen of my word processor. I also want to thank her for her assistance in translating between English and Spanish many times over the past few years.

A very sincere thanks to all of those folks who have contacted me through the website, attended my presentations on Family Scribe Groups, or enrolled in the Family Scribe Group seminar at UNLV. Your countless questions and suggestions demonstrated to me a clear need for a book like this one. I sincerely hope I have included everything you have asked about, as well as answered some of those questions you did not know to ask about when we met.

To my dear writing partners, Dennis Goode and Rikki Johnson, I know we have many more years ahead of us, writing by candlelight and sharing the stories of our lives over fried plantain and tears of laughter. This book had to be written, if only to prove that all our years of meeting as writers could actually add up to something on my part!

Special thanks to David Greenberg, award-winning children's author, for his enthusiasm and encouragement. I have had the opportunity to attend his workshops as a teacher, as well as have him in my classroom to work with my students. His love of words and writing is infectious, inspiring even the most reluctant of writers to engage in wordplay. I especially want to thank him for allowing me to describe how I have used one of his writing activities, the "I Know My Family" writing prompt, in this book.

I am grateful for the skillful talents of Sarah Graddy, who pushed me to refine and improve my ideas during the writing of this book. Her suggestions greatly improved the clarity and overall organization of this book's text and, in the process, helped me to formulate my thinking. Thanks also to Vera Goodman for her insightful reading and comments.

As you can see, the evolution and growth of Family Scribe Groups over the past years has been a collaborative effort. With so much active support, it is not surprising that we—the writers, students, and parents of the Fremont Family Writing Project—have succeeded as a writing group and community partner.

Introduction

Background

In 1996, I arrived in Las Vegas and two days later was teaching English at John C. Fremont Middle School, an inner-city campus situated between the Las Vegas Strip and downtown's Glitter Gulch. Like me, many of my sixth-graders were new to the city. They and their families had come to Las Vegas from Central and South America, Mexico, Eastern Europe, the Pacific Islands, Asia, and from cities all around the United States.

Urban Las Vegas, to these families, represented a starting-out point, a place to make new beginnings and to work at making dreams become realities. The city's immense service industry had job openings waiting for anyone willing to work. For the most part, these were low-level positions with long hours and strong physical demands. Since Las Vegas operates around the clock, seven days a week, parents, I quickly found out, were as likely to work the swing or graveyard shift as they were to have nine-to-five jobs.

Just as with a tourist's long-shot hopes at winning a big jackpot, much of Vegas' promise remains tantalizingly out of reach for new immigrants to the city, who find themselves stuck in low-end positions, struggling with multiple jobs without the education or language skills it takes to move up the ladder. At our school, the transient rate has passed sixty percent (the highest rate in the entire Clark County School District), a figure that reflects the searching and dream chasing that new families in Las Vegas' inner city undergo as a rite of passage.

Even in my first year at Fremont Middle School, I began to wonder if it would be possible to work directly with the families. A familiar chorus among some of my peers in those days was that it was nearly impossible to get parents involved in their children's educations. I hoped that parents would become more visible around our school if invited for reasons other than discipline conferences with counselors and deans. Our parents, I already knew, work hard and have full schedules. I guessed that in order to increase parental involvement at school we would have to develop some opportunities that were not threatening or directly connected to their children's academic day and which held some intrinsic rewards for the parents.

My most successful writing lessons in the classroom were those that gave my sixth-graders the chance to write about their lives, about their own experiences. These students' autobiographical narratives always resonated with powerful voices and compelling content. I had the strong suspicion that, given the chance, their parents would produce equally great writing of their own.

Besides my interest in exploring what sorts of writings the parents and children together would create, I really wanted the families to empower themselves through writing. I wanted to offer them a chance to punch an opening in the standard school setting and together say, loud enough for anyone to hear, "We are here, this is what we think, and we hope you listen." Voice and identity filled the community around my school, but I did not feel that those voices found many opportunities to be heard.

Occasionally our immediate community gained attention when a crime was committed or standardized test scores fell below average. Those stories just did not tell what, based on my experiences with my students and their families, I knew deserved to be told. To tell the truth, I found myself angry at the selective picture painted of my school and neighborhood. I wanted to see the families write about their own lives, in their own voices, and make those stories available to our surrounding community. I decided to start a Family Writing Project.

Early in my fourth year at the school, I brought my idea of creating a Family Writing Project to Dennis Goode, co-director of the Southern Nevada Writing Project. He immediately pushed me to bring the idea to Rosemary Holmes-Gull, Southern Nevada Writing Project's amazing director, who all but ordered me to create a proposal and a budget. Dennis and Rosemary saw the worth of my idea and would not let me back down. Their encouragement and commitment to my idealistic dreams pushed me to turn those dreams into something real, something that works.

At the same time, the City of Las Vegas began a neighborhood-based grant program, the Youth Neighborhood Association Partnership Program. Just as Rosemary and Dennis had seen the value in writing with families, the City of Las Vegas recognized that such collaboration between teachers, parents, and students would strengthen and enrich the city. Urban life, particularly in a city as varied and fast-paced as Las Vegas, too often severs lines of communication, making it difficult to generate a meaningful sense of community. We asked for a grant from the program and received $1,000 in 2001. That grant, and the ones the city has awarded us in subsequent years, validated our time together and reminded us to keep our project community-based, with real, visible benefits arising from our project for our surrounding neighborhood and its families, many of whom send children to the school.

I founded the Fremont Family Writing Project with families of students at John C. Fremont Middle School in urban Las Vegas, where I live and teach. Since then, teacher facilitators have begun Family Writing Groups with families around the city as well as across the country. All have used our initial work in Las Vegas as their starting model.

Our Fremont Family Writing Project took off quickly. Before we knew it, we grew not only in size but also in terms of the scope of our work. In this book, I explain how to facilitate the group at the heart of every Family Writing Project, which is the Family Scribe Group. We do have other activities organized under the umbrella term of Family Writing Project. For instance, some Family Writing Projects host after-school writing programs, which we call the After School Scribes, or organize community Family Writing Fairs. These efforts, along with Family Scribe Groups, can collectively form a Family Writing Project. The Family Scribe Group, however, is always the most important part of any Family Writing Project. Everything else centers on the Family Scribes. Most Family Writing Projects organize Family Scribe Groups without ever tackling these other activities. For more information about aspects of Family Writing Projects beyond Family Scribes, visit the Family Writing Project website at www.FamilyWritingProjects.com. In this book, the concern is solely with Family Scribe Groups.

Whether you are a teacher, counselor, social worker, church member, or some other professional who teaches writing or works with families, you will find that *Writing with Families* gives you everything you need to know in order to establish your own Family Scribe Group. This book will show you how to facilitate Scribe Groups that create writers, involve families, benefit communities, and inspire you in your role as facilitator.

Family Scribe Groups offer families the rare opportunity to come together and create a community of writers. Participants in these groups discuss ideas and issues that are important to them. They work together on activities, write extensively, and respond to each other's work. Many participants say that this experience changes their lives. Through Family Scribe Groups, children and adults gain leadership skills, find their personal voices, gain empowerment in their communities and schools, and become creators of a strong school–family connection.

This book is written for teachers and others who want to impact their schools and communities while growing professionally. For facilitators of Family Scribe Groups, the experience often affirms their professional goals. Teachers who lead Scribe Groups see that they can reach students; they exercise creativity and enjoy a level of autonomy that often does not exist in school systems. Without exception, all of the facilitators of Scribe Groups I speak with tell me that working with families on writing is one of the most inspiring and energizing experiences they have had as teachers. In fact, many say that facilitating Scribe Groups has kept them in the teaching profession.

School teachers are not the only ones who have used the ideas in this book to create something new and vibrant at their sites. Because of the community-oriented nature of Family Scribe Groups, the ideas and lessons presented here have worked in settings far removed from public schools, such as churches and parks and recreation departments. I have met family counselors who have told me that they hope this work reaches their colleagues because of the ways in which family writing, as a consequence of the communications it fosters, can influence the dynamics of family relationships.

Writing with Families gives facilitators a usable guide to designing and leading Family Scribe Groups. In this book, there is not only a detailed description of a five-week Family Scribe Group program that readers can adapt to their own needs and situations but also many more ideas for themes and activities that might be used in creating Family Scribe Groups. These ideas have been successfully adapted at sites across the nation.

How to Use This Book

Chapter 1 explains exactly what a Family Scribe Group is: how it works, whom it is for, and what it entails. It also gives eleven founding principles of Scribe Groups. Remember and follow these, and you will almost certainly facilitate a rewarding, fun, and exciting Family Scribe Group.

Chapter 2 offers thirteen steps in chronological order for preparing for your Family Scribe Group. Follow this checklist, and you should have everything you need to begin your first group.

Chapters 3-7 follow five weeks' worth of meetings in the life of a Family Scribe Group. These meetings can be spread out over a semester, a year, or whatever time frame works best for your group.

Chapter 8 suggests twenty-five different culminating projects that families might undertake to finish their work and recounts culminating projects the Fremont Family Scribe Group has undertaken in Las Vegas.

Chapter 9 provides a wealth of suggestions for themes and activities to use in designing your own Family Scribe Group.

Chapter 10 concludes the book by detailing the many benefits of Family Scribe Groups for students, families, teachers/facilitators, and communities. This chapter provides specific reasons why teachers would want to involve their families with this unique approach to writing and community-building on school campuses.

Finally, the **Facilitators' Resources** section is divided into five parts:

- "Benefits for Administrators" discusses the specific reasons why administrators will want to support Family Scribe Groups in their schools.
- "Sample Project" provides a sample five-week project plan, incorporating some of the themes and activities from **Chapter 9**, to follow or adapt.
- "Frequently Asked Questions" lists questions commonly posed to me at workshops and conferences over the years by teachers and others interested in Family Scribe Groups. My answers come directly from my experiences leading Family Scribe Groups and helping others to do so themselves. This is an excellent place to look for answers either before or after reading the rest of the book.
- "In Their Own Words: Facilitators Speak" highlights comments from experienced Family Scribe Group facilitators who relate how projects have benefited both them as professionals and their school sites. This section offers numerous anecdotes from diverse leaders, providing important peer feedback to those thinking about starting their own Scribe Groups.
- "Templates" includes project evaluation forms, assignment sheets, a release form, and other forms for facilitators to use, either directly from the book or as guides in designing their own forms.

I believe that, after reading *Writing with Families*, you will have a clear understanding of what a Family Scribe Group can mean to your site. You will have all the tools and ideas you need to guide and facilitate families through the process of becoming writers. Most importantly, you will feel the desire to become involved yourself.

1 What Are Family Scribe Groups?

*F*amily Scribe Groups are made up of families who meet, in order to write, with the guidance of one or more facilitators. Participants in Family Scribe Groups write about what they know best: their own lives. They explore the meaning of "community" in their lives through an overarching theme, such as "defining identity," and corresponding writing activities. During this process, families come closer together with other families. They always publish their writing to document their work and share it with others. Family Scribe Groups also take on some sort of community-oriented culminating activity or project, some work that benefits their communities and publicizes their efforts.

The role of a facilitator is to create situations that encourage a wide variety of meaningful, relevant writing while remaining flexible and attentive to the needs and interests of family writers. Facilitators, the leaders who guide the entire project, assist the family writers towards achieving all these goals through planning and leading activities that result in a variety of types of writing.

While writing is the main goal of a Family Scribe Group, much more goes on in a project than just putting pen to paper. Each week, the facilitators of a project prepare activities and prompts that will get family writers thinking. These might be art projects, such as drawing portraits or designing ceramic tiles that later will become part of a mural, or they might be conversation topics that the writers will discuss with partners or in groups. Eventually, however, all roads lead to writing in a Family Scribe Group.

There is no set formula to the writing, which assumes many forms. Sometimes the writing takes the shape of a list or the jotting down of notes. It might be a journal entry that later becomes part of a group poem or a story that reveals important memories or hopes for the future. *Everyone* writes at a Family Scribe Group, from young children to grandparents. And together, they share their written thoughts.

By the end of a Family Scribe Group, each family will have collected a portfolio of writings in their weekly binders. From their portfolios they assemble pieces to publish in a group anthology. Whether the anthology becomes a booklet, a CD-ROM, a website, or some other media form, it becomes the means of sharing a group's ideas and beliefs with others. It becomes a lasting artifact of what went on during the project. It also is a reminder for all of the family members of the time they spent in their writing community.

By participating in a Scribe Group, children and parents have the chance to gain an increased appreciation for writing. Many find that writing is something they want to continue after the group ends. They also discover ways of expressing thoughts and feelings that they may not have had an earlier opportunity or inclination to practice. In general, family members say that being in a Scribe Group greatly increases their interest in writing and awakens in them a desire to capture thoughts on paper. This is especially true for reluctant writers and members who tended to hold their feelings inside.

Parents or grandparents often come to the group because they have been invited or urged to join by a child. At the first class they expect to sit back and watch or to help their kids. With time, after a few activities and one or two writing opportunities, these hesitant participants become excited by the entire writing process. At first, they think they can excuse themselves from the writing. Eventually, however, they become writers and are as willing as everyone else to share their creations.

As you might have guessed, the benefits of a Family Scribe Group do not relate only to improving writing skills. Families become closer when they work together on activities dealing with relevant issues and ideas. When they write they share their feelings and thoughts, often expressing ideas that they have never before put into words. Parents look at their children with a new set of eyes. In a Scribe Group, children frequently take the lead, both with ideas and with writing. Parents often are surprised at aspects of their children's lives, feelings, and thoughts that come out through discussions and writing. The same is true for the children, who may discover sides of their parents that they did not previously know existed. For example, a mother might read aloud a paragraph shedding light on her behaviors as a parent. These moments have immeasurable effects on participants and by all accounts help to bring family members closer together.

A sense of community develops, too. Although the children in a Scribe Group might know each other from classes at school or time spent on a local playground, the families themselves are often strangers to one another. Through the Scribe Group, which deals with so many issues relating to family life and common values, families get the opportunity to increase their understanding of one another. On the one hand, families learn about the differences in their lives, such as those having to do with religion, foods, and holiday celebrations. At the same time, they learn that, despite many differences, they share underlying values. They all want what is best for their children, and they all care about where they live and their places in the community.

Family Scribe Groups generate a broad spectrum of exceptional experiences for family writers and teachers alike. Repeatedly, in their writings and discussions, parents and children point out features of Scribe Groups that they feel are crucial to their projects' successes. Similarly, teachers who facilitate Scribe Groups always identify elements that make their projects succeed. These elements are what matter most in designing and facilitating a Scribe Group; they are what make families excited to write and motivate teachers to work with families in such a unique setting.

It is important that facilitators of Scribe Groups take all of these principles seriously when designing their projects. They are not merely suggestions but rather factors for success that Scribe Groups share.

Principles of Family Scribe Groups

Remember that participants are families. A Family Scribe Group has families as its participants. Families come in many forms, shapes, sizes, and arrangements. Be liberal in your conception of family, and allow your members to define themselves. You will have to decide whether to allow children to attend without older family members, such as parents, uncles, and aunts. Maybe a student will show up with a neighbor or adult volunteer, such as a Big Brother or Big Sister. Usually, as word of your project spreads through your school or site, you will have children come to you to find out about joining. Some may not have adult family members who are able or willing to attend with them. It is difficult to turn any child away, but at the same time, your project is for families and much of a project's writing will derive from families' experiences. Be prepared to decide what you will do in that situation. Perhaps there is an adult at your site willing to work with a child who comes to the project without other family members; be open to other solutions.

Focus on families. First and foremost, a successful Family Scribe Group has facilitators who recognize that the group is for the families. Facilitators must remain flexible and be responsive to the directions in which families want to take their projects. The facilitator should not always be at the center but rather must step back and watch what happens when the ideas of parents and children move into the spotlight. A facilitator envisions situations and writing opportunities that give families a chance to explore and express their ideas but does not worry too much if those plans evolve into something quite different in the classroom. The facilitator also works alongside the families as a participant. Facilitators must write, share, and publish with the families. Just as importantly, they must listen to the families and respond to their ideas.

Recognize families as teachers. A child's first teachers are at home, not in a classroom. Throughout life, parents, grandparents, and siblings continue in their roles as teachers. In a Family Scribe Group, children work with the teachers who matter most in their lives: their families. These are the people who have spent years teaching right from wrong and sharing a wealth of knowledge beyond that imparted in the classroom. And families are the ones who will remain with students long after school days are over. Never diminish or overlook the value of bringing together families, not as your students, but as teaching and learning groups.

It is too easy for classroom teachers to assume that kids do not learn at home or to assert that students who are less accomplished at writing are victims of bad parenting. Scribe Groups recognize that every family is a repository of knowledge. There is an expression that asserts that each time an elder dies, it is as if a library has burned down. Parents and grandparents have knowledge far more expansive than any classroom teacher could ever pretend to offer. In a Scribe Group, the wealth of knowledge in family libraries finds expression in conversations and writing.

Appreciate that kids are people, too. Again and again, parents and teachers in Scribe Groups realize that the children in their projects are people. They have opinions and ideas; what they believe matters. Teachers realize this when they see children interacting with their families. Parents realize this when they hear their children intelligently discuss ideas and share their writings. Do not discount children's ideas and your project will certainly give each of them a newfound sense of worth and importance.

Let families shape your project's focus. The themes and activities of a Family Scribe Group must be relevant to the family writers. A Scribe Group is not the place for a facilitator, administrator, or other person in power to tout a personal agenda. Rather, the Scribe Group is a place where families have access to writing experiences that matter to them. It is from this clear sense of relevance that family writers will gain the motivation to write. It might be that the issues that matter in a Scribe Group are issues almost entirely overlooked or disregarded by schools or curriculum designers. Scribe Groups deal with lived experiences and knowledge gained from family life and with ways of turning those into writing. While facilitators might be experienced with styles or forms of writing, they must recognize that families are the experts of their own lives.

Create an accepting environment. It is crucial that participants of Scribe Groups feel like they are members and not just attendees. Every member must listen to others and realize that everyone in the group has unique contributions to make to the community of writers in the project. Facilitators must establish this attitude from the start. Acceptance might be stated implicitly in the diversity of cultures, ethnicities, or religions represented in the group's population at that first meeting. Or it may be represented in the variety of languages used by family members in their writing. Above all, a facilitator must emanate an attitude of acceptance and trust for the ideas, practices, and beliefs of their families. Otherwise, the enthusiasm and openness of the group will suffer. When everyone feels accepted and valued by the others, an almost magical sense of honesty and sincerity will express itself in every writing activity.

Give voice to the voiceless. Scribe Groups give a forum to individuals who might otherwise not express themselves or share their ideas. A father who does not often express himself well at home often will find words for his feelings in a Scribe Group. Students from marginalized populations, such as special education or second language programs, find their voices as they gain a place to write about their experiences to share with others outside their groups. Populations who lack political power or a strong voice in their school or community will find an outlet for their opinions and desires. For these reasons it is absolutely necessary that Scribe Groups publish their writing and share it with their communities and with each other.

Give writing primary importance. In a Family Scribe Group, writing is a revered activity, a treasured experience—anything but basic. A Scribe Group will turn to writing to interpret reality and define lives. Scribe Groups recognize that writing is a democratic activity that equalizes individuals and guarantees participation in the community. Everything in the group leads somehow to writing. Even if a family member does not share aloud what is on the page, there will be writing. And, without exception, facilitators practice what they preach and write alongside the families. Family Scribe Groups are an inviting way of promoting and encouraging writing among reluctant writers and of creating authors out of individuals who might never have realized the power of the written word in their lives. It is not difficult to see that a child's experiences in a group can shape how she approaches writing later in life, perhaps with her own children.

Measure success outside of given standards. A Family Scribe Group is not the place for curriculum designers to step in and say what is needed or for testing enthusiasts to discover ways to manipulate their statistics. Undoubtedly, there will be those who will want to see their work fall into alignment with state, district, or school standards and benchmarks. Others will feel a Scribe Group's success must be measured and quantified with decimal points and averages. Such aspirations have their places in public school programs, but these individuals entirely misjudge the business of Family Scribe Groups and fail to recognize a great deal of the achievements and successes that members will reach throughout a project. Find other ways to measure success, such as letting family members rate their self-perceptions as writers. Give everyone opportunities during a project to write about how they feel about their project and its attendant successes, surprises, and failures. These self-evaluations are the most important measures of a project's success. If you feel required to document a project's achievements for others—to school administrators or funding providers, for example—members should have a direct role in deciding what to share and how to compile that information.

Honor native languages. Allow family members to write and publish in their native tongues. By doing so you recognize that their native languages, as well as the language of the school setting, have the potential to communicate thoughts, feelings, and experiences. Also, keep in mind that literacy in a first or home language benefits literacy in second languages while also encouraging cultural and intellectual expression.

Balance mind and heart. Family Scribe Groups strike a balance between the intellectual and the emotional. Writing is an exercise of the mind that builds communication and language skills, but it is also a way of expressing feelings, dreams, and aspirations. Writing that is relevant to the families' lives will most often contain strong emotional content. It will reveal layers of participants' lives and uncover memories, ideas, and thoughts that may not have otherwise found expression. Facilitators will lead families into writing opportunities that have the potential for strong affective responses. There is, of course, the need to find ways of writing down thoughts and feelings so that others understand them, a need which falls more under the intellectual than affective domains. Here, the facilitator shares ideas and knowledge about writing, its various forms, and processes. The facilitator becomes, in a sense, the technical assistant aiding the experts.

These eleven founding principles combine to give your Family Scribe Group its purpose and identity. A project lacking any of them will probably fall short of its potential. As facilitator, it is your job to keep these principles alive as you plan for your project and meet with your families. It is also important that you model these concepts. Demonstrate respect for every member of your group, model good writing practices, and encourage everyone to participate. The facilitator role is less rigid than that of a traditional "teacher" who stands in front of the class, but it is every bit as important. A successful facilitator draws from participants their thoughts and ideas and creates a trusting environment that encourages their written expression. Keeping these principles alive in your project will go a long way towards helping you to achieve those ends.

2 How to Prepare for a Family Scribe Group

Facilitating a Family Scribe Group involves some planning and preparation. If you try to take care of a number of details before you actually meet with the families, your entire project will run more smoothly, and ultimately you will have to put less effort into the entire enterprise. The following checklist will help you get ready to work with your families. Note that it is organized in chronological order, not in order of importance.

Figure out if you need a partner. Before doing anything else, consider whether you will be working alone or with one or more partners. Many projects do fine with only one facilitator. I recommend, however, that you work with at least one other facilitator, at least in your first year. A co-facilitator might be a teacher or spouse, or you might ask one or more of the parents in your project to work alongside you each week.

You will be able to share ideas and reflect on your project together. This intellectual partnership is perhaps the most rewarding reason for collaborating. A partner, of course, also shares the planning and general workload which will make the entire process a little easier. Facilitating a Scribe Group should be a rewarding experience. So, rather than risk burnout, look for an enthusiastic partner (or two) whom you believe shares your enthusiasm for writing and who would appreciate working with families. I promise that anyone you involve will thank you in the end. But, even without a partner, you can greatly reduce your workload throughout the project by planning well before you begin.

Get administrative buy-in. This planning step applies whether you are doing your project at a school, through your city's parks and recreation department, at a church, or at any other site. You want to drum up as much support for your project as possible, even before it begins. At school, approach administrators far in advance of actually beginning to meet with families. An astute administrator will recognize that this project brings nothing but benefits. It involves parents and families, promotes academic learning, energizes teachers, excites students, develops community, and showcases the talents and creativity of the entire school community.

If administrators give you a green light to continue, ask them to help with materials, publishing costs, snacks, bottled water, and even teacher stipends. It may very well be that your project fits neatly into Title I grants or other sources of funds that your school receives. If so, your administration might be willing to fund some, or even all, of your project.

Find facilities. What facilities will be available for your use? Are you going to meet in a classroom, or is there another space, such as a library or meeting room, that would better satisfy your needs? Consider the size of your group. You want to create a sense of intimacy and community between the participants, so you should not use too large a room. Are you able to rearrange the seats or tables and chairs? I've found that seating families to face each other in a circle, semi-circle, or square works best. Avoid seating people in rows one behind the other or with their backs to each other. Eye contact and ease of communication between families and family members is important to establish through seating that encourages interaction. Remember that if you are meeting after hours, your group will need access to restrooms, pay phones, and other facilities.

Find financial and other means of support. It may be that your school or site is not able to support your project, either partially or fully. But there are other ways of finding the money and materials you need. Look for community-oriented grants. Many towns and cities offer grants to groups that improve neighborhoods or communities. Contact your city hall and inquire about such opportunities. There is also a strong chance that neighborhood partners will step forward if approached.

Visit local merchants, such as grocery stores and craft shops. Explain to them the type of work you will be doing with families in their community, and ask if they can help with in-kind donations. Many projects are able to depend upon the generosity of local businesses for all of their refreshments and many of their materials.

But do not limit your efforts to businesses only—it is quite possible that a nearby church or community service organization will pitch in as well. Often, these groups have to document the levels at which they serve the community around their site in order to continue receiving local, state, or federal monies. If you are located in their zones of operation, they are motivated to assist your project because they in turn are able to show that they are serving a larger segment of their communities.

Five hundred dollars should be enough to cover the expenses that will accrue during the course of the five weekly lessons this book outlines. The bulk of expenses will go to purchasing disposable cameras, developing film, and publishing the anthology. If necessary, trim those expenditures by using digital cameras, and look for alternatives to a traditional print anthology such as publishing on a CD-ROM or website.

Plan the specifics of your group in advance. It is a good idea to sit down and really plan the project. Remember to choose activities that correspond well with the theme you selected for your group. You can certainly use the five-week plan outlined in **Chapters 3–7** of this book, as many Scribe Groups around the country have already done with great success. Or, it may be that you want to come up with your own original project. If so, **Chapter 9** suggests themes and activities, and the **Facilitators' Resources** include another sample five-week project plan. You can also refer to www.FamilyWritingProjects.com for more ideas, examples of fully outlined projects designed by facilitators, comments from other facilitators, and general advice.

Even though you plan the project in advance, remember to be responsive to the families. There is always room to adjust and modify as you move through the schedule. In fact, such adaptations are part of the whole process. If you start with a good idea of what you want to do, you will be better able to make changes along the way. You will find weekly planning pages in the "Templates" section of the **Facilitators' Resources**.

Decide whom you will invite to participate. You want your project to be successful. Although you might feel you should invite everyone, groups that are too large lose intimacy and require more resources. I recommend that initial projects begin small. The groups will grow in size over time. Thirty (or fewer) participants is a good size to aim for, but don't be disappointed if you only have a dozen at your first meeting. Most groups begin with five or six families. Some families come in pairs, while others bring four or five family members. You can see that your numbers will add up quickly.

If you are a classroom teacher, take advantage of open houses and parent conferences to pitch your project to parents. Those who set aside time to attend such events at school are often the ones who make the time to become a part of a Scribe Group. Keep an eye open for students who love writing and who are excited whenever they set pen to paper, and ask them if they would like to join your group. It is better to look for students who will come eager to write than to invite every kid in your class and then deal with kids who really do not want to be at school after hours or on a Saturday.

Make a deliberate effort to invite a diverse cross-section of families. The Scribe Group should ideally represent the demographics of your school or site. Many of the greatest writing opportunities in a Scribe Group will deal with community and the similarities among, and differences between, members of your community.

Design your schedule. Will you meet after school, in the evenings, or on Saturdays? When will facilities be available for your group? Look at a calendar and schedule your entire project in advance. Send copies of this schedule to your families with their initial invitations. They need to know dates well in advance so that they can add them to their already busy schedules. When you first meet with them as a group, discuss the schedule and see if it needs to be modified.

Most Scribe Groups meet for two hours per meeting with at least ten hours of contact time from the beginning to the end of their projects. With fewer contact hours, a project's sense of community does not develop adequately. A Scribe Group could have more contact hours, but most follow a schedule of five meetings spread out over a semester. I follow that pattern in this book and for that reason, refer to each set of activities as a "weekly lesson." If a class lasts only an hour, don't rush through the activities. Instead, spread a weekly lesson over two sessions.

Contact families prior to the first meeting. Inviting the families once is not enough. Remain in contact with them between the initial invitation and your first meeting so that they do not forget or make other plans. It is easy to keep families involved—the trick is to get them to show up for the first meeting. If there is a long period of time between the initial invitation and the project's beginning, plan to send home several reminders. For example, you might make phone calls to families as the project nears. The week before your first class, send home invitations that say "You're Invited to a Party!" or something similar. Store-bought party invitations work well. In these days of e-mail, it is fun for kids and parents alike to receive invitations through the U.S. Postal Service. You also can send home a letter that requires the parents or guardians to sign and then return if they plan to attend. This commitment is not binding, but it does help.

Consider the languages of participants. Now that you have a general idea of who is going to attend, do you need to think about adjusting your project for speakers and writers of languages other than English? If you know that you will have Spanish speakers, for instance, is there a way for you to translate letters home or assignment sheets and writing prompts into Spanish? Are there bilingual speakers to translate and help out during class? These might be facilitators but could also be members of the families. For example, children might be able to translate for their parents.

Think about publicity. You will want to have releases available at your first meeting. These are important if you plan to create an anthology or to otherwise publicize your event in the community or on the Internet. It is only fair, and quite possibly a legal requirement, for you to receive signed releases prior to publishing any work that family writers create as part of the group project. The

"Templates" section of the **Facilitators' Resources** has publicity releases that you can use. The school district or site might have other publicity releases as well. At the first class session, explain that signing the releases is optional, but important, if family members want their writings to be published or shared outside of the class.

Create a supply list. This is a general list of supplies that Scribe Groups use regularly. Your project may not use all of these, but you will probably use most of them.

- Invitations and envelopes
- Name tags
- Three-ring binders
- Wide-ruled notebook paper for the binders
- Pencils and pens
- Colored markers, crayons, and colored pencils
- Colored butcher paper and poster board
- Bottled water
- Snacks such as chips or cookies
- Overhead projector and transparency sheets
- Computers and printers
- Disposable cameras

When planning your budget, consider whether you can obtain some of these materials through donations or from your site. Also, decide whether you will undertake a culminating activity, described in **Chapter 8**. Other supplies not listed here may be needed.

Invest in a digital camera, if possible. Most projects document much of their work using digital cameras. You might take pictures for your anthology, to put on a website, or for a display at your site.

Prepare binders. Put together a three-ring binder for each family. In the binders, place release forms, wide-ruled notebook paper, a tentative schedule of the entire project, and a note signed by the facilitator(s) welcoming them to the Scribe Group. Keep these binders with you, rather than letting them go home, so that you are able to keep track of all the writing that goes on. You may want to make photocopies of writings between meetings, and you will want to have the binders at the end of the project when it comes time to publish your Scribe Group.

If possible, take a photo of each family at some point during the first class. Digital pictures are definitely the easiest for this purpose. Slip this photo under the clear plastic cover of the binder so that when they arrive at the following classes, they have personalized notebooks.

Figure out how you will publish writings. Decide, either before your group first meets or soon after, how you will publish the group's writings. Traditionally, most Scribe Groups have created small runs of anthologies, usually printing enough for each family to receive one copy with a few extras for facilitators, administrators, and other interested parties. Families love to have copies to keep and show off. Print anthologies are also something you can share with your peers and use to publicize your project in your community.

Copying costs, however, can be prohibitive. Too often, publishing an anthology becomes the main expense in a Scribe Group's budget. In Las Vegas, Scribe Groups are increasingly looking for other, less expensive alternatives of publishing their work while still reaching a broad audience.

Before you begin your project, inquire as to whether your school or site will pick up printing costs for an anthology. Look for alternatives if you do not have the money available to publish a print anthology. Maybe you can publish on the Internet, particularly if your school already has a website. Look for a place in your community, such as a public library, grocery stores, or businesses where writing, photos, and artwork can be displayed.

With technical support, publishing your writing on a CD-ROM is another low-cost alternative. Visit www.FamilyWritingProjects.com to see how other projects have presented their work online.

3 Week One: Getting to Know Each Other

*T*he main goals at the first meeting are to break the ice, to introduce ourselves and to write about our new friendships, defining our group in the process. Follow these plans and by the end of the day you will have written a group poem, done some journal writing, and established bonds that will last throughout your Family Scribe Group.

Agenda

- Welcome/sign-in/binders
- Snacks
- Artifact sharing
- Group poem #1
- Thirty-second interviews
- Fill-in-the-blank poems (homework for Week Two)

Welcome/Sign-in/Binders

In my Scribe Group, facilitators make it a point to see that everyone who participates signs our attendance sheet and grabs a nametag. At the first week of each project, members find journals they can take home and keep. We always make sure to have boxes of pens, pencils, colored pencils, and markers, just so that we can be certain our group is ready for any writing situation that arises.

The sign-in sheets remind us who showed up each week, and they also are valuable when applying for grants since they record the size of our project and when we have met. I strongly recommend that you keep accurate attendance records so that later you are able to document your work.

As families come in, each receives a binder with the family's name on it and notebook paper inside. These binders are used throughout the Family Scribe Group's time together to safely store all of a family's writings. To prevent the binders from getting lost, you can store them at the site until the next meeting. At the end of the five weeks, families can, of course, keep their binders, but be sure to make copies of writings you would like to save.

Snacks

Never overlook the power of offering simple snacks. Some of the kids who have been through our groups come that first week because they know there will be chips, juice, breakfast bars, or donuts. Our facilitators bring these snacks to the first couple of sessions. Usually by the third week, the families offer to bring food from home to share and possibly to write about.

Artifact Sharing

Included in the invitations and letters sent home each year before we meet for our first time is the request that each person bring along one or more items to share with the group. These should be artifacts that reveal aspects of the bringers' personalities and identities so that all of us learn something about each other right from the start.

Once everyone has signed in and has their refreshments, we sit in a large circle to introduce ourselves and share the personal items brought from home. Although some of the kids might know each other from school, much of the group will usually be strangers to one another. Some of the parents are wondering at this point what the project is all about. Families are sitting together but not really talking to each other. All of that is about to change with the artifact sharing.

First to share is Julie, a mother who has brought with her four of her five children, ranging in age from five to seventeen. She beams proudly as she holds out a silver Olympic coin from Salt Lake City, a souvenir from the family's trip to the Olympics. She also wrestles with several bulging family photo albums as her kids squirm in their seats, afraid she will show us embarrassing snapshots. She doesn't, but she does finish by saying, "Family is who you are and what you stand for," which draws applause from everyone in the group.

After her turn ends, it's time for her children to stand up and show what they have brought. Elisa, an eighth-grader, shakes several snow globes from her collection, including one with the unlikely image of a blizzard burying the Las Vegas Strip. Her brother Jonathan, in his first year of high school, smiles and turns a light shade of red as he shows a worn-out stuffed animal, a frog that he received as a kid. He explains to us all that he collects frogs of all kinds and has since his early childhood.

We move around the circle. One mother at first passes her turn but then stands up and says she has brought with her the most valuable possession in her life, her daughter. She cries as she speaks about loss, about how her own childhood was not always happy, and how she wants so badly to give her daughter a happy upbringing. She is divorced now and confesses to us that she is afraid she may be failing her daughter. Across the room, another mother responds by saying that life moves through changes, that she had been in the same position but now has a caring husband and a job of her own and is creating a safe home for her own three children.

Everyone pays close attention to each presentation. Children hold up colorful autograph books signed by friends, a game-winning football, action figures, video games, and even dinosaur bones unearthed on a family trek to the desert. By the time we have all shared our artifacts, a change is obvious. We have made connections, and emotions—ranging from laughter at a child's nickname to tears over a teddy bear from a mother's first date with her husband—have swept around the room. Artifact sharing is glorified "show-and-tell" that gives us entry points into each other's lives. To make this a truly meaningful kick-off for our writing project, we need to reflect.

Group Poem #1

Each year we write one or two group poems. This first group poem activity, which grows out of artifact sharing, is important because everyone contributes a line or phrase. The poem represents all of us and is our first attempt at writing as a community.

After making our way around the sharing circle, we take five minutes to write in our journals. The prompt we use is simple: "In your journals, write down some words, ideas, or feelings that come to mind when you think about the items we have just shared and the people we have just met."

Some parents and adults dive right in, their pens seemingly driven ahead by thoughts. Others are hesitant. It may have been years since some have been in a classroom, and others have likely never written anything to share with others. Quite magically, silence falls over a room that moments before had been filled with stories, shouts, laughter, and tears. And, most impressively, it is our students, the children, who are leading by example, demonstrating the same excitement to write that they put into action in their writing classes during the week. As a facilitator, you will find this moment, when parents and children first write side by side, as equals, exhilarating.

As everyone finishes writing in their journals, we regroup to share ideas. Once a number of members have read, we ask each person to pick out a word, phrase, or sentence that strikes them as being somehow important. Then each is given a large strip of paper on which to copy what they have chosen from their writing.

What follows next is often one of the most memorable activities of the entire group. We invite everyone to gather around the strips of paper on the floor.

Together the families organize the strips into a coherent poem. This activity involves everyone. We read through various versions of the poem until we all agree that it has reached its finished form.

Here is the group poem written by our third-year Fremont Family Scribe Group.

"The Family is Important."

The Family is important
In many different ways.
Some strive to be better,
Others play all day.

Dalmatians, Frogs,
Toys and dolls.
Elmo, report cards, robots,
Pictures from the past—trying to remember
What it is like as a sixth grader.

Emotional responses, promises,
Diversity, and always, the main idea—
Family is important to us all,
Yes, family is important.

Other kids and families
May seem different than mine,
But they are all alike in ways,
We're all one big family.

Life experiences are different,
But somehow, still the same.
Old, young—but still,
Everyone likes the same,
Loves the same.

Fathers, daughters,
Pain to joy,
Mothers, sons, far away.
Close to the heart,
Connections and memories,
Family and friends,
Oh, so many memories.

Some have it harder than others.
Many emotions fill our hearts.
Adults have more to share,
Different places and lifestyles.
We carry special things inside to remind us,
We're not alone,
But united as one.
Love and Peace reign forever in our hearts.

Love your family,
Forgive and forget,
Find the love of God.
Memories, teachers, wonderful parents,
Beautiful children, togetherness.
Loving, caring.

I love school, it's a place to learn,
Hearing different stories about each other.
Many families that love and care about kids.
Warmth, closeness, unity.

Everyone has something special,
Special to them in their own ways.
Everyone here is on the same page,
From different backgrounds, but we are here
For the same reason, the children.

From the poem, deliberately left rough, several key ideas that are guiding forces behind our Family Scribe Group leap off the page. Of course, there is the idea that families are important. Some families have two parents, others a single parent, foster parents, or a neighbor who steps in to fill a void in a child's life. In any case, they are families, and they understand that their support and love is a source of strength. Also, there is the idea that differences between the families, although important, do not erase the beliefs or emotions they all have in common. It is worth all the effort it takes to stage a Family Scribe Group just to hear some of these ideas come from young children and to see the wide eyes of parents as they listen to such wise words from their young people.

Some of our parents have commented during later weeks of Scribe Groups that one of the most valuable lessons learned is that the families do have so much in common. This poem brings out that point but not at the expense of individual and ethnic differences. We celebrate those too, yet both children and parents immediately see that there are similarities within the differences.

Very little editing is ever done to these group poems. We leave them as diamonds in the rough because they capture so well our individual and collective voices. This method for composing a poem might tempt an editor's pen, but we pretty much leave the poems the way they landed when dictated. A strong aspect of this type of spontaneous poem's appeal to our group's members is that the poem comes straight from their journal reflections. Everyone has a line or phrase in the poem that is his or her own, and together these combine to create a group poem that contains us all. At our second class, everyone gets a copy to keep, and we read it aloud as a group.

Thirty-second Interviews

Now that we have gone around the room and shared our artifacts, it is time to break the ice and meet face to face. For these interviews, we divide the class into two groups—children and adults—and ask them to sit in two long rows facing each other so that each student is paired with an adult partner.

In this activity, the facilitator reads one prompt at a time from a list of short questions and statements. Each person has thirty seconds to "interview" the person across from him or her. We want everyone to get to know each other just a bit more than they did through the artifact sharing. This activity is always a hit with families. They genuinely enjoy the interviews, and the brevity of each response somehow intensifies the experience.

The interviews begin with the parents asking the first question to the children across from them. After thirty seconds we repeat the question, this time with the children asking the adults. Before moving to a new question, however, each child moves down one seat, putting them across from the next adult in the opposite row. Then, after each has asked and responded, one side of the two rows moves down a seat, bringing together new sets of partners.

Basic questions such as "What is your name?" and "Where were you born?" begin the activity. Questions farther down the list such as "What do you look for in a friend?" and "Where do you see yourself in ten years?" are more challenging, especially considering that each person has only a half-minute or so to come up with an answer.

Here is a full list of one set of questions we have used that work well.

What is your name?
Where were you born?
What is your favorite movie?
What is your favorite food?

What was/is your favorite subject in school?
Describe your best friend.
How would your best friend describe you?
How do you describe yourself?
What do you like about your city?
What do you like about our neighborhood?
What is your funniest memory?
What is your most prized possession?
What was your most embarrassing moment?
What makes you scared?
If you could live anywhere, where would you live?
Where do you like to go when you travel?
What do you look for in a friend?
Where do you see yourself in ten years?

Halfway through the list, we mix things up by having some of the parents sit on the side with the kids and some of the children switch over to what had been the adult side of the two rows. Now, instead of only parents asking kids and kids interviewing parents, we also have parents interviewing each other and children asking questions of one another.

This activity begins with a level of seriousness and perhaps a little tension. After all, talking to strangers about life issues is not something that most of the kids do often, and everyone is trying to be polite. A few questions into the interviews, attitudes begin to change. Because it's difficult to squeeze replies into thirty seconds, everyone finds himself or herself talking quickly and forgetting to feel uncomfortable. By the middle of the activity, do not be surprised if everyone is laughing and shouting. Kids will jump to the next seat and parents will greet one another with smiles that invite new friendships.

After finishing the interviews and settling down a bit, we take ten minutes or so to scribe in our journals in response to the prompt, "Write about what you've learned about others, yourself, and our new community of writers during your interviews."

This opportunity to write is our second foray into our journals of the day—not bad for our first session together! The interview activity brings up so many ideas and involves everyone with so many other group members that no one flounders without ideas for their journal writing. Not surprisingly, many of our writers responding to this prompt focus on how friendly everyone seems and on how much they seem to have in common with them. Of course, they come from different parts of the country and world and have different favorite places, but their basic underlying values are very similar. As one student said, "We all want friends and family that we can trust. Everyone here seems like they could be my friend."

Fill-in-the-blank Poems

Our first week gives everyone a chance to share and learn. In designing a homework assignment for the families, I wanted to come up with something that would build on the ideas expressed through artifact sharing and the thirty-second interviews. It was also important to remember that many of the parents have not been in a classroom for years and may not speak much English or consider themselves writers. The fill-in-the-blank format for creating a highly personal poem works extremely well. It does not require much time or effort yet produces unique and personalized works from each participant. (The poem is brief enough that you can probably design templates in other languages, if need be. You can find a Spanish version you can use in the "Templates" section of the **Facilitators' Resources**.) Everyone gets a copy of the poem template as homework, and we promise to let everyone read their poems at our next class.

Notice that each line of the following template contains an idea that we have already talked about, either in the artifact sharing or the thirty-second interviews.

(Name): _____

From _____.

Who believes in _____,

And loves _____.

A person who would like to have _____,

Visit _____, and _____.

(Name): _____

A person who has fun when _____,

Whose funniest memory is the time when _____,

And whose most prized possession is his/her _____.

(Name): _____

A person who loves to eat _____,

Who is embarrassed when _____,

And who wants friends who _____.

(Name): _____

(Three adjectives describing yourself): _____, _____, and
_____.

With that, Week One comes to an end. We have all stood up and shared artifacts and the stories that give them meaning. We have sat across from each other, asked questions, and listened to ideas and feelings. We have written in our journals twice, and we have created a group poem. Awfully productive for a Saturday afternoon when the rest of the school is empty!

Depending upon your situation, the ages of your students, how much time you have to meet, and how much you want to achieve, you may find that this first week's lesson plans, or the ones for following weeks, are just too much to cover. The biggest factor will probably be how many people are in your group. Our first year, we had thirteen people at our first class and there was plenty of time to cover everything. The Fremont Family Scribe Group has grown so much in three years—we often have up to 50 attendees in our first week—that we are lucky to finish the artifact sharing, do journal writing, come up with a group poem, and go over the homework. Be flexible, and you will find that these lessons will motivate your group to write and, at the same time, inspire you as a teacher.

4 Week Two: Where We've Been, Where We Are

W eek One's activities established group closeness and familiarity. The second week explores more fully the group's theme, which, for the Fremont Family Scribe Group, was defining our identities as Las Vegas families living at the center of this marvelous, confusing, and ever-changing city. I believe that the activities in this chapter will work for you whatever your location. Week Two's discussion has to do with where families live and work, and the writings deal with memories and life in the present day. These issues are ones that families everywhere can identify with and write about.

Agenda

- Welcome/sign-in/binders/snacks
- Review of group poem (from Week One)
- Fill-in-the-blank poems (homework from Week One)
- Brainstorming and journal writing—our community
- "I Remember" and "I Know" poems
- Homework assignments

Before going too far into Week Two, I want to write a few words about what you might expect from this week. We've learned from experience that group membership will grow throughout the five weeks. Do not turn families away because they missed the first week. It seems that every year, one or two families who had encountered scheduling conflicts the first week turn up at our second meeting. Also, word will have gotten out, and it's inevitable that a kid who before had not seemed interested will now want to join. Emphasize to any child who wants to join after the first week that this is a family group, so he or she should bring a parent or an adult guardian.

Welcome/Sign-in/Binders/Snacks

Every week begins in the same way, with the sign-in sheets, Family Scribe binders, and a snack table. Prepare a few extra binders for newcomers. New families are likely to need some time during the opening minutes to complete the project-related paperwork. To make this time productive for the other families, consider beginning with an opening prompt, something that ties in with the day's theme. You might ask them to list places they have lived or to jot down a few thoughts on how they feel about where they live now. If there is a piece of writing from your last meeting that you want everyone to have, such as a copy of your group poem, include it in the binders along with the weekly agenda and any other schedule concerns, such as reminders of upcoming meetings.

Reading the Group Poem

Reading the group poem from Week One is a magical way to begin the second class. Not only is the poem posted in the room on our strips of paper from Week One, but it is also printed out and included in the Family Scribe binders, with a title and perhaps some organizational touches added by students during the week. (As a classroom teacher, it is easy for me to give the group poem from Week One to several of the Family Scribe Group children with instructions to type it on a computer, making minor revisions as they go.)

Their product is a real poem, a black-letters-on-white-paper poem that everyone can hold in their hands and read aloud—which is just what we do. As a group, we read through the piece, with children and adults vying for a chance to read a line or two aloud. The group poem reminds us all of who we are as individuals and as a group. It also helps to introduce us to the few new members who have joined the group.

Do not overlook the chance to read group work aloud. The experience affects everyone in the room. Kids and parents will both feel pride when they hear others reading their words. At the end of the reading, there is a moment of silence while the children's eyes are still on the paper and the parents contemplate their words. That moment before anyone claps is a calm silence that says more than any applause could.

Expect clapping to follow once everyone has caught their breath. We always recognize our writers by clapping after they read their works. This recognition is important and encouraging.

It seems that every year, after we have read the group poem aloud, a discussion about our group and about why we are here in school on a Saturday seems natural. One father in our first year said that it gives him a chance to spend time with his daughter, who he barely sees during the week. A mother in that same class said, "I'm here because it gives me a chance to share in my daughter's childhood."

Hearing some of the children make comments like "writing is fun" has an impact on the parents. How often do parents get a chance to not only go to class with their kids but to listen to their children talk about how much fun it is to do what looks suspiciously like schoolwork? Probably never. The children's excitement clearly inspires the adults and gives them reason to admire their kids.

Fill-in-the-blank Poem Homework

The fill-in-the-blank poem assigned for homework the previous week is so easy to write that it does not intimidate many people. It is also is a form of poem that lets writers express their own personalities, likes, and dislikes. Maybe it is for those reasons that, almost without exception, everyone who has taken the form home in the first week has brought it back filled in and ready to read in the second week, year after year. Other facilitators who have used this writing assignment say the same thing. Often, they are surprised that a homework assignment comes back with one hundred percent completion. I am not surprised. The first week raises enough issues and touches on enough aspects of identity that it seems reasonable to think family members would want to further describe and define themselves.

Here are several of the poems group members have written. First, a poem from Dess Garcia, an original member of the first Fremont Family Scribe Group with her son Patrick, from 2001 :

Dess,
From the Philippines,
Who believes that hard work, patience, and perseverance
will always be rewarded,
Who loves her family and to sew, cook, and do crafts.

A person who would like to travel,
Visit Germany and Canada, and to make new acquaintances.

Dess,
A person who has fun when on vacations with her family,
Whose funniest memory is the time when her youngest son smothered his face with
his cake on his first birthday,
And whose most prized possession is her family.

Dess,
A person who loves to eat seafood,
Who is embarrassed when asked to talk in front of people,
And who wants friends who understand her.

Dess,
Kind hearted, Loving and Understanding.

In 2002, Dess joined the Crestwood Elementary Family Scribe Group in Las Vegas with her youngest son, Phillip. Then, in 2005, she joined the Fremont Scribes when Phillip entered middle school. It is exciting to see a parent participating in three different Las Vegas Family Scribe Groups; this phenomenon points to the potential for growth among groups.

Julie E. Kofford and her daughter Elisa have stuck with the Fremont Family Scribe Group since its first meeting. Here is Elisa's fill-in-the-blank poem from 2003. (Elisa is also known to friends as "Bean.")

> *Elisa Bean,*
> *From Illinois.*
> *Who believes in doing what is right*
> *And loves to be with someone who will make her laugh.*
>
> *A person who would like to become a famous writer,*
> *Visit outer space, and have many friends.*
>
> *Elisa Bean,*
> *A person who has fun when she is laughing with her friends,*
> *Whose second funniest memory is the time when she got a sticker up her nose,*
> *And whose most prized possession is her dog, Lucky.*
>
> *Elisa Bean,*
> *A person who loves to eat sweets,*
> *Who is embarrassed when she makes a mistake,*
> *And who wants friends who will listen to her.*
>
> *Elisa Bean,*
> *Crazy, Fun, and Smart.*

These poems make a great follow-up to our first activity of the day, reading the group poem aloud. Everyone in the room finds a chance to contribute. Our first week's activities made us all feel comfortable with each other. Now, in the second week, it is not hard to stand up with a fresh piece of writing and deliver it with a little more self-confidence. At first, a few group members, usually parents, listen to others read with rapt attention but look down at their hands when it is the next person's turn to read. By the time those who are most anxious to be heard have had their turns, the more reluctant sharers are usually ready to give it a go. I really cannot remember a single writer in my last Scribe Group not sharing aloud during this activity.

Brainstorming and Journal Writing

Las Vegas is a one-of-a-kind anomaly in this country. It is a city founded upon and dedicated to creating a fantasy setting for the world's tourists to descend upon and enjoy, often engaging in pursuits they do not indulge in back home. There are, of course, areas of the city without casinos, neon, streetwalkers, or twenty-four-hour drinking, but these areas are far from Fremont Middle School. If you have been to Las Vegas, you have seen the 119-story red neon needle atop the Stratosphere Hotel and Casino tower, and you have probably driven down Las Vegas Boulevard past wedding chapels, live peep shows, and fantasy motel rooms. The Stratosphere tower sits well within the zoning boundaries for Fremont Middle School, as does the neighborhood beneath it, known as Naked City for the showgirls who used to sunbathe in the nude by day before donning feathers and jeweled skullcaps for dinner shows on the Strip. Every card dealt by a dealer falls onto a green felt table in a Fremont Street casino in or next to the Fremont Middle School zone. Lower Fremont Street's once-popular motor inns are now half-shuttered motels with empty pools—home to families new to Las Vegas who pay rent by the week and send their kids to Fremont Middle School.

The Fremont school zone is an odd gerrymandered creation that, on paper, looks like an elongated lizard. Somewhere around that lizard's midsection is a quiet, established neighborhood with homes priced well beyond a teacher's budget. There are other, more modest middle-class neighborhoods, some with lawns and well-kept backyards and others with paint peeling off houses and desert weeds. And there are dozens, if not hundreds, of old and new apartment complexes advertising low move-in rates scattered throughout.

Along with this diversity in neighborhoods and homes comes great ethnic diversity. Spanish-speaking families from throughout Latin America dominate as the newest force in our zone of the city. Families from throughout Asia and the Pacific Islands arrive daily. African-Americans make up about eleven percent of the population, with whites measuring in at twenty percent of the mix.

As you can imagine, kids growing up in this cultural hodgepodge encounter influences and obstacles that other kids around the country just do not see on a daily basis. I have not visited any other city where kids waiting at a bus stop behind their middle school will pass at least half a dozen newspaper machines vending free copies of full-color pamphlets advertising, in decidedly immodest poses, "Blondes, Asians and College Girls, Naked to Your Room" and not even pay attention! For them, that is life in Vegas.

The week's theme, "Where We've Been and Where We Are," lays the foundation for our prewriting activity, which is a whole-group discussion of our community's role and place in the Las Vegas Valley. After talking for a while about our neighborhood and lives in Vegas, we brainstorm lists of likes and dislikes about our area of the city, then read them aloud. Here is one group's list:

Likes	Dislikes
Hoover dam	Rude people
Old, big trees	Pornography on flyers, taxi ads, newspaper machines
Peaceful atmosphere	
7-11s and convenience stores	Helicopters overhead
Ethnic foods	Crime, drugs
Good schools	Graffiti
Hardworking teachers	Traffic, car accidents
Sense of history	Hot, hot weather
Cheap food	Air pollution
Semi-tropical plants	Bad food
Rock art	Temptations: gambling, alcohol
Beautiful weather all year	Uncaring people
School music program	Trash in the streets
View of the mountains	Bad bus drivers

After compiling the lists of likes and dislikes, which a couple of students quickly scribble on the overhead, we all take a few minutes to write paragraphs in our journals. Sarie Barnett, a thirteen-year-old author who penned a hundred-page mystery novel before finishing middle school, sees both the good and the bad in Las Vegas. As she reads aloud, her voice rises and falls to accent her cutting observations about a child's life in the inner city.

"Las Vegas, Sin City or Our City?"

Las Vegas is a very unique city. It has its up and down times. I mostly like the warm weather, the cheap food, and all the exciting places we can visit. Some say that we live in Sin City because of the gambling, inappropriate pornography in the streets, and all the violence. I guess you can say those people are right.

Vegas is known for the bright lights and the joy on people's faces when they win at gambling. That happens a lot. When some

people arrive in Vegas it is like they are arriving in heaven. Yes,
it is a cool place, but that's just one side. Parents don't think
their kids see everything, but in Vegas, we do. We see pain and
heartache, tears and blood. We see things that we will always
remember, things that can put fear in our eyes and hearts. I guess
I might be sharing too much of the truth, but I could win a Vegas
jackpot if I bet you that in one day you can find drug dealers,
homeless people no one cares about, drunk drivers and maybe even
a dead body in one of our busy intersections. Maybe that is whey
they call it Sin City.

Maybe if we all worked really hard as a community then we would be
able to get rid of all of this sin in Sin City. It's not the government's
fault, but ours. After all, we families do live here. Without us, you
can't make a city, right?

Sarie always tells things like they are. Her writing is true and gutsy. When she shares her observations with our families, there are lots of heads nodding around the room. Once again, it is one of our children opening the eyes of adults and gaining their respect through the written word.

"I Remember" and "I Know" Poems

These two poems mine the memories of our adult writers and encourage the younger writers to express what they know of their lives today. Author and presenter David Greenberg deserves thanks for teaching me the "I Know My Family" prompt. Before using this activity with our Family Scribes, I had seen him use it effectively with both teachers and students.

To begin the writing, we divide our class into two groups. The children stay in the classroom with one facilitator, the adults move to another classroom with the second facilitator, and neither group knows what the other is going to write. If you are facilitating on your own and are not able to divide the group in two, you might want to lead both the children and their parents through the "I Know" poem without worrying about the "I Remember" piece. Parents have as much fun with the "I Know" writing as do their children, and after all, you cannot be in two places at the same time, even if you are a veteran classroom teacher.

Both groups are going to write poems about childhood. The adults will think back to when they were the ages of their kids, of the places they lived, the people they knew, the games they played or maybe the food they ate. The kids are going to write about what they know about their families.

Working with the parents on this particular poem is fun because they get to practice the entire writing process, from brainstorming to final drafts. I begin by telling them that I am going to lead them through the creation of these poems just as if I were in my middle-school classroom working with students. The parents get a kick out of that idea, as well as the topic. I begin with a poem I have written about my own childhood called "I Remember":

I remember dinnertime,
My father just home from work, alone in the living room swaying to Frank Sinatra,
My mother in the kitchen banging pots and pans, calling us to the kitchen table,
And me slouched on the couch, reading the sports page and comics,
Avoiding my math homework.

I remember big family dinners on loud birthdays and colorful holidays,
Steam on the kitchen window,
The slam of the oven door and the excited high-pitched tone of children's voices,
Aunt Naomi up to her elbows in Deviled Eggs, Uncle F.J. telling terrible jokes.

I remember breakfasts before school,
My brother Kevin complaining about the powdered milk,
My mother on her cooking stool, frying eggs,
Telling us that someday we will appreciate how she woke every day to send us
off with food in our stomachs. She was right.

I remember corned beef and cabbage on St. Patrick's Day with boiled potatoes,
Heath Bar cakes on my birthday,
Turkey drumsticks and rich brown gravy at Thanksgiving,
My brother Tim's vegetable tempura deep frying in smoking oil,
and chicken tetrazzini on Sundays when my father cooked.

I remember these meals and foods from my childhood,
And I feel my stomach growl!

After reading the poem and sharing it on the overhead, I show them an idea web that I made before writing the poem, the kind of idea web that I expect my students to create when we practice brainstorming. When creating my web before class, I consciously include elements of good writing craft, such as descriptive words and strong images. I ask the parents to point out ideas on my web that catch their attention and then show them how I used them in my own poem. Hopefully, after my example, they will intentionally include similarly powerful imagery in their own webs and poems.

Before I can finish moving around the web to cover all of the ideas, some parents are already working in their journals. One father's web reaches across two pages, then spills across the backs of both. He looks up as I walk by and says to me, "It's incredible how much I can remember. I could write a whole book of these ideas." At another desk sits a grandmother who had originally agreed to join this group with her grandson without realizing that even she would have to write. She looks hesitant and glances around with a slightly embarrassed and nervous expression. Around her are a dozen adults scribbling away in their journals, barely taking the time to look up.

"I don't know what to write about," she says.

I tell her that my sixth-graders often say the same thing. When they do, I advise them to write about what they know. This grandmother, who was born and raised in Las Vegas, must have plenty of memories about how things have changed around her in the past decades. I suggest she think about some favorite place of hers from her childhood, some place that is gone now. A few minutes later, I look over and see her filling in an intricate web with ideas that seem to grow across the page.

"Can we start on the poems now?" a mother asks, her page marked with circles and cursive scrawls.

I had planned to talk more about how to take the ideas from the web to create a poem, but now I back off. The parents are getting the idea pretty well on their own! For the next half-hour, everyone in the room is writing, giving me a chance to check in on my co-facilitator, Kim Sicurella, and the kids who are writing poems about their lives in the here and now.

Our students, of course, are pros at the whole brainstorm, rough draft, writing-process thing. To them, it's old hat, but at the same time they really want to impress their folks with their finished products, so it turns out that they are taking their time. I thought that it would be the parents who would proceed slowly, but in the other room the parents are already moving their lips as they silently read their pages and whisper to each other about what they are writing.

Mrs. Sicurella has a different prompt for the kids but has asked them to draw up idea webs, too. Her prompt is "I Know," and she asks the kids to focus on what they know about their families. The poem she wrote and modeled for the students is called "I Know My Family":

"I Know My Family"

I know my nephew…
His hungry cry and content laugh
His smell after a bath.

I know my family.

I know my mom…
Her generous ways
Her contagious excitement
The smell of gardenias
"Oh my!" and "Really?"

I know my sister…
The baker, the mom, the glue,
Her detailed lists,
Her overly organized ways,
Her chocolate chip cookies.
"Ugh, I have so much to do it's not even funny!"

I know my family.

I know my brother-in-law. . .
Overbooked and hungry,
Begging for something sweet,
Tennis, darts, basketball
The Rolling Stones.
"I was thinking…"

I know my family.

The students love the theme of this poem. If there is anything they know, it is their families. On their webs they have bubbles drawn for each family member. Connected to these are more bubbles filled with mannerisms, behaviors, and quotes. The level of excitement in the room contrasts with the studied, calm approach of the adults. One girl is so sure she has pegged her mother in her first draft of the poem that she is grabbing the shoulder of the student next to her and forcing her to listen to what she has written. A boy who usually writes short, concise pieces, grins a bit devilishly as he moves past the middle of his page, and he does not bother to look up when I sneak a peek over his shoulder.

We have to rush the kids a little bit in order to stay ahead of the clock, but it all works out. Back together as a group, we prepare to read aloud and hear them chant, "Can I read?" and "Can I go first?" Of course you can.

With the two groups back together, adults and children share what they've written. This poem from Anne Packingham is simply titled "For My Son John":

> *In my past, is a child who ate ice cream on the lawn*
> *on a hot summer's night,*
> *Who fished on the pier and was amazed by the ocean*
> *in the dark of the night.*
>
> *I remember being young,*
> *looking for bottles all day to cash in.*
> *The money was for Sunday drives, the length of which always*
> *Depended on how many bottles we collected.*
>
> *I remember picnics in the park,*
> *The whole neighborhood in the public pool,*
> *My parents listening to the Beatles when no other parents would,*
> *Everyone dancing at our house because our parents were cool.*
>
> *I remember waking and slipping from bed,*
> *My bare feet on hardwood floors*
> *While the scent of night blooming jasmine*
> *Filled my head.*
>
> *Now as your mom, you don't need to wonder*
> *Why I plant jasmine by your window and*
> *As you fish in the lake, I look*
> *Like I might cry.*

Adults sharing these poems in class have a right to feel proud. Their writing is genuine and sincere, and it tells important ideas to their children about who their parents are and were.

Homework Assignments

It is your call whether you decide to assign homework or not. With this group, homework assignments let us squeeze in a little more work than we can finish in our two hours and also are a way of creating a sense of continuity. Homework can work as a prewriting activity as well, setting up the writing you want to accomplish in later weeks. That is the case with the homework everyone takes home at the end of Week Two in the Fremont Family Scribe Group.

Each family receives a manila envelope with two assignments inside. The first of the two is nothing more than several sheets of graph paper with instructions to draw maps with representations of houses and neighborhood landmarks. The adults are to draw the places where they grew up, where they lived when they were the ages their children are now. We ask the students to draw maps of where they live now. Neither set of instructions is overly explicit, and both sets give everyone plenty of room for interpretation and imagination.

The second assignment comes with a disposable camera. We have already talked about our community and the aspects of community life here that we like or dislike. Now the families have the chance to take pictures around the neighborhood, capturing images of scenes that are important to them. They might take pictures of high-rise hotels, their favorite convenience store clerks, or their bedrooms. Las Vegas may be one of the most photographed cities in the world, so it just makes sense that we look at it through our own lenses.

The map assignment will be due when we meet at our next class. Everyone has a couple of weeks until we will use the photos, but as I will develop the film for them, I ask them to see if they can get the cameras back to me at the next class.

Both assignments, drawing the maps and taking pictures around the community, are ones that should work for you, wherever you call home. Maybe your families will not snap shots of the world's largest casino or of the Las Vegas Strip at night, but they will find places and things that hold meaning for them. You can find both of these assignments in the "Templates" section of the **Facilitators' Resources**.

5 Week Three: Building a Community Starts with Family

W eek Two led the families through an investigation of their community and gave them a chance to write about it. Now the focus shifts to the past as the parents get the opportunity to share places and childhood stories. The children have the opportunity to share images and ideas from their own lives. In Week Three, everyone also will put into writing their own interpretations of the slogan "Building a Community Starts with Family." This writing activity takes the form of an exciting balloon game and follow-up journaling that leads to the creation of a second group poem.

Agenda

- Sign-in/binders/snacks/journal writing
- Map sharing and storytelling
- Balloon game

Sign-in/Binders/Snacks/Journal Writing

Journal writing is a good use of time at the beginning of class while waiting for all the families to show up. We use journal prompts at the beginning of class to review past ideas and set a theme for the current week. Journal writing also helps to bring thinking back to the group in case it has been a while since the last meeting. Prompts we have used at the beginning of Week Three include:

> *What have you gotten out of this group so far?*
> *What has it been like for you compared to your expectations?*
> *What might the benefits be of continuing this group in the future?*
> *How do you think we impact our community?*
> *What would you want to tell others about our Family Scribe Group?*

It is hard to tell who leads the way when we are writing, the kids or the parents. In one corner of the room, two mothers listen to their children as they explain their opinions before beginning to write. The mothers nod encouragingly, say a few words, and then open their own journals. At another table, a mother reads the prompts with her sixth-grade daughter and second-grade son. It looks like she is guiding them through the questions, but really, the daughter is helping her primarily Spanish-speaking mother with the English wording of the questions. This challenge seems to motivate both of them, and the mother asks if she can try to write her ideas in English.

"I might need somebody to read it to help me make sense," she says, before laughing. "It's the first time I've made something like this in English."

The grandmother who confessed the first week that she is not much for writing is one of the first to finish a page in her journal. It seems nothing can stop her, but then she taps her grandson on the shoulder and asks him to read something on the page. She points to the page with her pen, and he reads what she has written. Then he nods approvingly and gets back to his own writing. One family wanders in late, sees everyone writing or talking about his or her ideas, and takes a place at an open table. Without asking any questions, the mother and two children read the questions on the overhead and hunch over their journals to begin work.

In all, we take only about twenty minutes to write in our journals, with most of that time spent while waiting for everyone to arrive. The time for writing is brief, but it is obvious from the depth of the ideas expressed in their writing that the prompts have struck a chord.

From the Perera family come two entries, one in English and the other in Spanish. From Ivette, the daughter, comes a short piece she calls "Writing is More Fun Than Anything at All for Us":

> I think our project is important because it helps us to get along with each other. We learn about parents, teachers and kids. I also think parents and teachers don't know enough about their kids, and that the project helps them to learn about them.

Her mother, Guillermina, writes:

> Este proyecto es importante porque nos entretiene y nos enseña cómo compartir con las demás personas, les enseña a los niños a participar y a desarrollar sus ideas, y así los mantiene ocupados.
>
> (This project is important because it is entertaining and teaches us how to share with others. It teaches the children to participate and to develop their ideas. At the same time, it keeps them occupied).

Elisa Kofford, a student who began with us as a sixth-grader and has continued with her younger brothers and parents for five years of the project, writes:

> *To me the writing project is a place to get to know people better. It's a place where feelings, emotions, and memories happen. It's a place where you feel love from everyone, and it's a place where great things happen.*

Another of the mothers, Shaunene, writes:

> *This writing project has made an impact on my family and me from the first day we attended. Within the first hour, our group came together in an incredible way. As we shared about ourselves and our goals for this project, everyone opened up in ways that engendered interest and empathy in both the students and adults. One of the most important benefits of this project for me as a mom is that I'm getting to know my children better through their writing. After we leave each project meeting, we have a discussion about our writing, and anytime parents and their children can communicate it is a great thing. The Fremont Family Scribe Group builds a great bridge from the school to the community.*

Map Sharing and Storytelling

Everyone has brought with them drawings of various shapes and sizes demonstrating a wide range of artistic abilities. The kid's drawings are of their Las Vegas neighborhoods, of the areas that they know best around where they live. The kids tend to place their houses at the center of their maps and then mark places like schools, churches, stores, and main streets. A few of the children choose to ignore the outside world and focus on their homes, emphasizing their own bedrooms and yards.

The parents' maps show pueblos, rural towns, Pacific islands, and faraway cities that they have left behind physically though not mentally. The map of one mother from a small pueblo in Southern Mexico shows blue rivers that wind to white geysers exploding in the mountains. Another mother has drawn a small box at the center of her map representing the trailer she grew up in as a kid in the Carolinas.

We make transparencies on a printer in the classroom and let everyone take turns at the overhead showing their maps and sharing whatever stories have come to mind. Kimberly Rafferty, a parent, puts her transparency on the overhead and smiles.

"I grew up in a little town just east of Orlando." She points to a simple map showing a couple of roads, square shapes representing several houses, and scattered trees. "Up here is my house, on about seven acres. We actually had a doublewide trailer. These are trees," she says, pointing to tree shapes drawn like inverted brooms. "It's different here than in Florida because there you actually have to remove trees to build a house. Here, we hope we can grow them!"

Her map shows where her first boyfriend lived and the path to the house of her childhood best friend. There's a field where she and her neighbors played football in the rain and a cornfield where her junior-high-school band would camp for three nights each year and "shuck truckfulls of corn for the corn festival."

In one corner of the map is a general store where they sold "barbecue and produce," a "post office and library in one," and the church where, she says, "we all went." Pushing back her hair and turning to face her map projected on the wall, Kimberly produces a sheet of notebook paper and announces, "I've written a little poem about it that I call 'Memories of Youth.'"

Liquid sunshine and
Lemonade stands,
Playing with friends
On beaches with clams.

Loyal pets and
Mile walks,
The smell of orange blossoms
We picked during serious talks.

The smell of sweet corn
And hot butter,
This memory stands out
More than any other.

Three days shucking
Truckloads of that corn,
Camping out with friends
On sleeping bags worn.

Memories like these
Will be cherished forever,
Of being kids, young loves
Growing up together.

She finishes reading and everyone applauds. Kimberly removes her map from the overhead projector and heads for her seat, wiping at what looks suspiciously like a tear under her right eye.

Becky Jensen, one of the group's few parents born and raised in Las Vegas, reflects on the city's growth when she shares her map with us. She has a drawing depicting the Las Vegas of thirty years ago, before there were six-lane surface streets and strip malls.

"This is my neighborhood, not too far from here really," she says. "There are two little 'X's on the map. The top one is my parents' home, and the 'X' on the bottom is my family's home, where we live now." The map shows a few streets, a small island of houses, and little else. It sure is not the Las Vegas of today. "This is what I wrote about our neighborhood because this is what I remember," she says, before beginning to read in a clear, measured voice:

> As we drive down Lamb Boulevard the kids like to say, "The cone patrol is out again." There is so much construction on Lamb lately, especially in front of Home Depot. As my grandmother used to say, "My, how things have changed."

> Flashback to 1975: My brother and I used to drive from the church on Stewart and Prince Avenue to Chaparral High School every morning for school. It was interesting because Stewart ended just east of the church and we had to drive on a dirt road the rest of the way to reach Lamb Boulevard. Then we traveled south on Lamb. Lamb was a small narrow two-lane country road.

> There was nothing but desert east of Lamb and just a small pocket of houses between Stewart and Charleston on the west. There was nothing until Parkdale, the few houses then behind Boulder Station, which was then just the site of the Skyview Drive-In Movie Theater.

> I clearly remember making this drive one early morning in the spring. As is usual in Las Vegas, it was rather windy. As we traveled south and reached the area just south of the wash, we were in the midst of a sand storm. It was blinding and we had to drive slowly to even see the road. The sand was coming from a graded area of land just east of Lamb. This construction site was to be a new neighborhood of homes. We thought how strange it was to build a subdivision in the middle of nowhere. Our parents bought one of those new homes just a few months later.

> The construction in front of the Home Depot now is interesting because I remember how thrilled we were when they first put a bridge over the wash. Of course, we couldn't drive through it, and unlike some residents in Las Vegas today, we had the good sense not to try. We had to travel east to Nellis to travel north because Nellis was a four-lane highway.

*Even though it's very convenient to have a grocery store right
around the corner and a Wal-Mart not too far away, I miss our old
neighborhood. There is just too much traffic congestion and people,
for the most part, are extremely rude and inconsiderate on the road.
The growth of Las Vegas hasn't slowed, no matter the economy
of the nation. On the contrary, it seems to be growing at a faster
and faster rate. It makes me wonder that if Las Vegas has grown
so much in the last twenty-five years, what kind of growth will my
children experience in the next twenty-five years?*

Living in Las Vegas is a continual exercise in future shock. In one of the nation's fastest growing cities, landmarks are swallowed up and forgotten. Becky's essay really catches everyone's attention and sparks a discussion about old Vegas.

"It's changed a lot," Becky says, with wide eyes. "I went back home to Florida for Christmas and nothing had changed," Kimberly Rafferty comments, laughing.

Balloon Game

A banner on the wall reads "Building a community starts with family." It is a simple idea that sums up our entire enterprise. To begin this activity, everyone receives a small strip of paper several inches long and no more than an inch wide. On the paper, each writes a phrase or idea of his or her own that responds to the one on the banner. They might reword "Building a community starts with family," jot down a memory it triggers, or respond with their own phrases about family or community. Next, everyone rolls up their strips of paper, pushes them into balloons of different colors, and fills the balloons with air.

We push the desks out of the way, or, if it is not too windy, we step outside. We all stand in a circle facing one another, each armed with a balloon. At the word "go," pandemonium breaks out. Blue, yellow, red, and green balloons arch into the empty space between us in a sudden splash of color. Before they touch the ground, our circle shifts. One boy grabs at a blue balloon that he chases across the floor and then bats into a father's beard. A mother with a camera ducks too late as a green balloon tossed by her son bounces off her forehead. Across the room, a mother chases after her daughter with a red balloon that she spikes like a volleyball.

As the burst of activity slows, each person picks up a balloon of a different color than the one that they had inflated at the beginning, the one into which they had hidden their strips of paper. The objective now is to pop the balloons and retrieve the messages, which is, for some, easier said than done. One father resourcefully pops his balloon with a ballpoint pen, while around him kids are stomping on their balloons with mixed results. In the end, however, we all salvage the secret messages and head back to our seats to read the notes aloud: "Build and they will come," "Building families brings communities together," "Family dinners," "Planting seeds for the future," "Find me first, and then you will find yourself," "It takes a village to raise a child," and "Families make community."

We are able to use the phrases in two different ways. First, we stand in a circle and read them aloud, one at a time. As we speak, a student at the overhead arranges the lines into our second group poem. Next, each of us uses the phrases from the popped balloon as a prompt for journal writing.

Here is the group poem made up of ideas inspired by the phrase "Building a community starts with family" in our first year of the project:

> *Families Make Community*
> *It takes a village to raise a child*
> *Find me first—*
> *Then you will find yourself.*
>
> *Life is a precious thing with family…*
> *Family dinners, everyone talking at the dinner table,*
> *Quality time like this keeps families together.*
>
> *Los fines de semana nos reunimos familiarmente*
> *En diferentes lugares, parques, o en la casa de alguien.*
> *Cocimos carnes or maíz, hicimos tamales.*
>
> *Strong families make a strong community,*
> *Strong families create responsible, productive citizens.*
> *Raise children with love, and they will become loving adults.*
> *Family is community—*
> *Community is family.*
>
> *Positive growth in Las Vegas starts with family.*
> *Cooperation with new friends and family, working together to make a happy community.*
> *Families can help the community.*
> *It takes more than one good family to make a great community.*
>
> *Planting seeds for the future.*
> *Build and they will come…*
> *Building a community takes friendship.*
> *Uniting families brings communities together.*

This group poem is really nothing more than a collection of phrases from the balloons. Like our first group poem, it contains ideas from all of us. It is a true community work.

After reading the phrases as a poem, everyone goes to their journals to write, using the messages from our balloons as a prompt. One boy, who started with the phrase "Growing in Las Vegas starts with family" on a strip of paper in front of him, writes a short piece in which he points out how hard it is for one kid to make a difference. He observes, however, that when we come together as a community of families, positive changes inevitably occur. His comments echo those of Sarie Barnett in her essay "Las Vegas, Sin City or Our City?" Written for our previous meeting, her piece recognizes that our community benefits from family involvement and honest discussions about life in Las Vegas. Both children see that it will take community efforts—like our Family Scribe Group—to begin influencing how people think about their lives in such a potentially daunting setting.

After writing and sharing, we are finished with Week Three. As the families leave, we remind them to return disposable cameras given to them at the end of Week Two so that we can get them processed. With three weeks down and two to go, our group is growing closer and coming to know a lot about each other. This closeness will strengthen in Weeks Four and Five.

6 Week Four: Where Are We Now?

Week Four emphasizes the present, the here and now. Photographs taken around the community are used as prompts for discussion and writing. We also find writing topics in foods brought by the families to share. Writing about the foods gives family members the chance to tell stories and share food memories.

Agenda

- Sign-in/binders/potluck
- Writing about and sharing food
- Sharing our photographs in groups
- Writing about our photographs

Sign-in/Binders/Potluck

What do the following foods have in common? Fried *taquitos de pàpa,* homemade pretzels called "horse legs," southern-style boiled peanuts, double-cheese scalloped potatoes, kiwi cream cheese pizza, macadamia nut cookies, stir-fried collards, cinnamon-topped *buñuelos, patacones* (fried, green cooking banana), Mongolian beef, *moros y cristianos* (black beans and white rice), mom's macaroni and cheese, homemade cream puffs, tortilla pinwheels, and Filipino pancit noodles. No, they are not dishes on the brunch menu at a Las Vegas hotel buffet! These are some of the foods families have brought to share with their classmates.

Writing about and Sharing Food

Our community partners have usually been able to finance or supply most of our snacks and drinks throughout our projects. But variety packs of chips just do not compare to the fare our families can cook up. Usually by the fourth week, we ask the families if they are interested in bringing food to share. We suggest that the recipes be ones that have some special meaning or which are family favorites. We have, in some years, shared food as early as the second week, though we usually save writing about the food until Week Four.

Hosting a potluck lunch not only guarantees good eating but also sets up our first writing prompt of the day. While everyone is filling their plates with food and settling in around the room, we point out a few questions on the overhead projector:

> *What does the food you brought say about your family?*
> *Can you remember any family stories having to do with food or*
> *   family dinners?*
> *What traditions does your family follow that have to do with food?*
> *What foods do you love or hate?*

After a short discussion of the prompts, we begin the real work at hand. At one table, two mothers silently lean close, elbow-to-elbow, their pens moving rapidly across their pages. Although around them parents and kids are still going back and forth with plates in their hands or sitting in conversation at their seats, neither seems to notice. Young Kaleb Kofford, only four years old, sticks out his tongue as he slowly shapes letters into words, one simple sentence to a line. His mother Julie splits her attention between her own journal and Kaleb, somehow writing several pages while helping him craft his four or five sentences.

Now five minutes into journal writing, most of the conversations have died away in deference to writing. There are still stragglers with paper plates sneaking cookies and fruit salad, but they make it back to their seats without much delay. Latecomers to class see the others writing, grab a plate for themselves, and open their Family Scribe binders.

At one table, a twelve-year-old girl lists her favorite foods while beside her a friend works out a rhyming poem about macaroni and cheese. At the next table, Ivette, an 11-year-old, holds up her notebook above a plate of home-baked cookies to show her mother what she has written so far. It takes a moment to get her mother's attention away from her own writing, a short piece about green enchiladas and potato taquitos, two of her family's favorite foods.

While at times there is as much nibbling as writing going on around the room, we all eventually have pieces ready to share aloud. Kim Sicurella, one of the group's facilitators, shares a story about her Italian father, who was famous in her family for shouting out, "While you're walking through the kitchen, stir the sauce, and don't forget the middle!" It is obvious from the laughs, smiles, and applause that our group appreciates her story and the fact that she, as facilitator, wrote alongside them and shared what she wrote.

There are times in the classroom when teachers do not feel they have the time to write with their students, or teachers may not think it is important that they write—after all, it is the students working for the grade, right? That kind of thinking has no place in a Family Scribe Group. We are all writers here.

Kaleb Kofford is at first reluctant to read aloud in front of so many big people. Seeing that he is intimidated, his mother volunteers to go first and reads a piece about foods of her childhood, about making homemade spaghetti sauce with her father, a recipe handed down from her great-grandmother. She also reads her memories of yearly smelt runs, when her family, "along with hundreds of others, would be off to the shore with nets and buckets." Then they would have fish fries and a contest to see who could eat the most.

"We always took off the tails and set them aside to eat last. They were the best, nice and crispy," she says. Julie concludes her piece, "Food represents fulfillment, comfort, and just plain fun for our family."

She finishes reading, and her middle son Jordan jumps in with a short essay detailing some less than delicious dinners he and his siblings have suffered through at home. His story causes his mother to squirm uncomfortably, but she admits that a few recipes have gone wrong. Four-year-old Kaleb has watched them both read and heard the applause and laughter accompanying their efforts. Now he has the courage to read aloud with a little guidance from his mother who points along the page with her pencil and helps him with a few words:

> *I like to eat spaghetti. I like to eat Ramen noodles. I like to eat macaroni and cheese. I do not like fried eggs. I do not like broccoli. I do not like tomatoes.*

Before he can sit back from his journal, our whole group breaks into applause and cheers that leave Kaleb smiling bashfully at his success as a writer. There is no doubting the sense of confidence and boost to his self-esteem that writing and sharing aloud has given him.

Another reluctant reader, Joann Lowe, is volunteered by her husband, who leans comfortably back in his seat to watch her at the center of attention. She doesn't back down, however, and after casting an ornery "I'll get even" grin his way, reaches for her journal, her smile softening by the first words of her story:

> *Food memories are many for me because, you see, I love food. My greatest childhood memory is remembering my mom telling my brother and me, 'Don't eat all the food. I made it for <u>the people</u>.*

Joann emphasizes her mother's command by striking the tabletop with her left palm and leaning forward toward her surprised grandson. A second later, she throws her head back and laughs along with the rest of us at his startled reaction. After catching her breath, she continues:

> *After the company left, then mom would tell us, "Eat all that food before it goes bad!" The donuts by that time were getting hard. Later on, my brother went into the service. When he came home on leave mom had all kinds of goodies made for him. I remember he would sit at the table and look at me and laugh and say, "Hey, I'm one of the people!" So now it's become a family joke in our house whenever people come over, our nieces or nephews, or whoever, we say, "Don't eat all that food, it's for the people!"*

Sharing Our Photographs

Plates pushed aside, it's time to look at the photos we took with the disposable cameras passed out in Week Two. Every family has a roll of shots they have taken around our neighborhood and throughout Las Vegas. A few have even brought along bulky photo albums brimming with family photos.

We break into groups of two and three families each, and immediately the room fills with laughter and voices as photos are dealt out like casino cards for everyone to see. At one table three families crowd close together, their eyes all focused on a picture held by a mother, who beams as she says, "This is a photo of the Country Inn, the first place my husband and I went out to eat after we were married, as a married couple." Spontaneous clapping and cheers erupt, even before she finishes speaking. Next to her, another mom holds up a photo of all her kids piled over one another on a couch. "I took one of them because nothing's more important to me than my children. They are why I'm so rich in life."

Across the room another cluster of parents and children huddles closely. One boy anxiously waits his turn, a close-up shot of a panting dog held in his right hand. He has time to kill, however, while his mother explains a photo of her doll collection, a collection she began as a young girl in the Philippines.

In another group, loud laughter explodes and a daughter runs across the room where she stands laughing and covering her face with both hands. She blushes as her mother holds up a picture of a toddler's swing set and explains that her daughter, now too big for the swing set of her childhood, "got stuck in the swing and couldn't get free." Gales of laughter rise up as the daughter fans her face and ducks behind a chair, hoping to hide her embarrassment from the group.

There are photos of smiling best friends, shiny new cars, pet dogs and cats, churches and temples around Las Vegas, neighbors in their yards, hangout spots, casinos, parks, and backyards. It takes a while for everyone to find opportunities to share, but after half an hour we are ready for each group to pick out a few photos to show off to the entire class.

Eva smiles shyly as she shows us Chino, a cat who is more "people" than feline. Another girl, Felecia, brandishes a snapshot of her friends from fifth period. In the photo, four laughing girls fall forward hugging each other, their eyes dancing for the camera.

Kimberly Rafferty brings a serious note to our sharing as she holds up a photo she and her daughter took "just around the corner from school." In it, three abandoned shopping carts lie haphazardly in the street and across the sidewalk in front of a cinder block wall. She explains that when she first saw them strewn there she realized they represented a "part of living where we do in Las Vegas. Too many times when we see something like the shopping carts, we have the tendency to ignore it and move on." This fact of life in our community is heartbreaking, she says, because people from other parts of the city, "when they are in our little part of town, expect to see things like this, which is sad. Cars and people go by," she adds, "without even noticing what is in their own neighborhood." Her photo of the carts is in our first anthology, along with a caption: "Seeing these shopping carts brought me a feeling of sadness because people see things like this and act like they're not even there."

Once each group has had the chance to share several photographs, we move on to writing about the images. On the overhead, I show a few prompts:

> *What common ideas do you see in the photographs?*
> *What differences do you note between families' photos?*
> *What important themes did you see in the pictures?*
> *Were there any surprises?*
> *What do these pictures that you took say about YOU, here and now?*

I also show a couple of examples I have written, poems based on my own school picture from sixth grade. One is a haiku, and another is a poem repeating the phrase "reminds me of." I make it clear that all these questions and prompts are only good "until something better comes along."

Fifteen minutes and a slice of cake later, just about everyone has wrapped up and we are ready to read aloud thoughts inspired by sharing our lives through photos. One main idea, which just about everyone points out, is that while our photos showed how every person and family in our group is unique—one family lives in an apartment, another in a house they designed—certain common themes and images are clear.

As one mother eloquently expressed it, "The same things are important to us, although we are all from very different backgrounds." A father added, "The real surprise here isn't the differences, it's that we are all so much alike."

Of course, the idea of this activity is not to try to gloss over the cultural or ethnic variety our writing project represents. The photos make many of those differences very clear, whether they are found in the churches the families attend, the restaurants they like to frequent, or the places they like to go when they have family time together. It is important that we all appreciate and value our individual and family differences. At the same time, the families cannot help but note and comment on the fact that the values underlying the differences they find between each other are very much the same.

Parent Dess Garcia makes salient observations about our similarities and differences in her paragraph:

> After seeing all the pictures that members of the Fremont Family Writing Project had taken, I noticed that all the pictures had a lot in common. Most of the pictures focused on family and religion. We may come from different families and cultures, but we all have the same concerns regarding the safety of our neighborhood. We all want to raise good kids and make them succeed in their lives and be useful citizens of tomorrow.

Eva, a sixth-grader from the project's third year, wrote about clouds captured in a photograph snapped by her classmate Christina:

Clouds remind me of big people who float in the sky all day.
Clouds remind me of spirits watching over their loved ones. I hope my great
Grandparents are watching over me.
Some people say they are just big balls of air and gas.
I think they are other people just like us, upside-down, and what we are really
looking at is their fluffy white cotton underwear.
You might think it's funny, but it isn't.
You couldn't begin to imagine what is up in the sky.
There aren't just birds and bugs.
From the sky you can see all the world,
People below looking back up in a sunny park, eating hot dogs.
You can feel the wind going through your body.
Not to mention, they are pure,
not a spot of dust.
They are always up in the sky moving past the sun.
Anytime they don't come out I am sad, but
I know it is for a good reason,
like a spirit council!

Maria, a sixth-grader in the project's first year, snapped almost all of her photos around her house, in the kitchen, in her bedroom, and in her yard. Our first anthology has three of her photograph writings. One is a haiku, another is an acrostic poem, and the third is free verse.

"Closet"

Hangers with nice clothes
Modern, hip, stylish wardrobe
Shoes, skirts, shirts, pants fit

"Hammock"

Hanging by two poles
A bed swaying in the breeze
Mounted atop pepples
Making you sleepy
On it, rest dormantly
Cradles you to relaxation
Keeps you in dreamland

"Our Kitchen"

A place where we stop scouring
Get away from chaos
And start devouring
Relax, chew, watch T.V.
Spending time with each other
Becoming a family

As a final activity with the photographs, we briefly discuss what we have seen and heard, then summarize our ideas about the photos, stories, and journal writings. On the overhead we create two categories, "Common Ideas" and "Important Themes." Religion, the importance of family, stores and restaurants, and backyards all fall under the first heading. We list family, religion, pets, home, memories, and fun as important themes. In the end, one mother sums up the entire session when she says that through stories, photographs, and time spent with children at activities like this, "We plant a seed in our children, hoping that it will be fertile and grow."

I believe that this camera activity, as well as the potluck and writing about the food, will work just as effectively at your site to inspire conversation, the sharing of ideas, and good writing as it has for our group. Both activities deal with universal themes and ideas. Everyone has favorite foods or recipes, and everyone can remember a story having to do somehow with food. The same goes for taking pictures and sharing them. While not everyone loves to have their picture taken, just about everybody will have favorite places to photograph or knows of something in their neighborhood that others will find worth looking at.

By now, everyone will be able to see how much the group has grown since the first meeting. The group has matured, not only as writers, but also as a close community of friends.

7 Week Five: The Future

*H*aving moved through the past to the present, now it is time to consider the future. In this week's activities, everyone will write a letter to themselves. But there's a twist—we postdate the letters ten years in the future. As this is the last meeting of the group, we also take time to thank each other and to recognize one another's contributions to our group, again through writing. This time, everyone writes thank-you notes expressing what they have gained and learned from one another.

Agenda

- Sign-in/binders/potluck
- Sharing earlier writings
- Future-letter writing
- Friendship notes
- Wrap-up and discuss culminating activity (see **Chapter 8, "Culminating Activities"**)

Sign-in/Binders/Potluck

As in Week Four, our fifth class begins with a buffet of world cuisine prepared by our families. Polynesian flan, deviled eggs, Mexican tuna fish, Filipino egg rolls, green cilantro rice, and St. Patrick's day cookies are a few foods laid out on a table along the wall. We do not write about the foods this week, but we do listen to a few family stories about the dishes.

Sharing Earlier Writings

Because this is our last time to write and read together, we give everyone a chance to look through their Family Scribe binders and pick out notes, poems, and paragraphs to share aloud.

Future-letter Writing

Future-letter writing is an activity that always stirs deep emotions. During our previous classes, we looked at the past through maps, recipes, and stories. We examined the present with photographs and writing about where we live now, in modern Las Vegas. In future-letter writing, our future lives become the topic of thought.

For this activity, there are two prompts, one for the parents and one for the children. The parents write letters to their children, imagining that the kids are receiving the letters ten years in the future, when they will be adults in their early to mid-twenties. The students also write letters, not to their parents, but to themselves as they hope to be.

Everyone seems to find this topic easy, at least at the beginning. Pens and pencils run across journal pages almost without hesitation. There comes a point, however, when parents re-reading their words begin dabbing at their eyes or blowing their noses.

An amazing moment during our first year of the Family Writing Project occurred when Nikole, an eleven-year-old sixth-grader, read aloud her letter. In her message to her future self, she asked whether she had published a book of poetry yet and whether or not she had found a husband and started a family. Nikole's older sister Jill, who at that time was a high-school student, was with our group for the first time. Listening to her younger sister wonder about her future had a strong impact on Jill. Before Nicole had finished reading the letter she had written to herself, Jill broke into uncontrollable sobbing.

Once she was able to speak, Jill confessed to the group that while listening to Nikole read her dreams and hopes, she realized, for the first time, that her sister was growing up. She had always thought of Nikole as a kid getting in the way of things. Now she saw Nikole as a mature, thinking person. The two sisters embraced and neither fought back their tears as they said how much they loved each other. Everyone in the room realized that sharing these letters with our community of friends can be life-changing.

Their mother, Becky, wrote this magnificent letter to the two of them that day in class:

My Dearest Daughters,

How very proud I am of you. Jill, you have grown to be such a beautiful woman. I really enjoy attending your performances and concerts. You play the piano so beautifully and you sing even better. I especially enjoyed your performance in the opera company's production last month of Madam Butterfly. And I was so proud to read that the critics thought you wonderful as well.

Nikole, your talents, although not as public, are as great and wonderful as Jill's. I keep your first book of poetry by my bedside. Whenever I feel down or depressed, it gives me joy to read your beautiful poetry. I am so proud of you and of your accomplishments as a writer. I know you will be graduating from college soon as a teacher and I know that your students will love you.

Do you remember that writing project we participated in at Fremont when you were in sixth grade? That was the first time I knew what a great writer you were.

Girls, I've talked about your accomplishments in the professional world, but I think what I am most proud of is what loving, thoughtful, caring wives and mothers you are. I love to have my grandchildren visit. They are so happy, content and secure. I know that they come from homes where love is the most important thing.

I look forward to writing again in ten more years. I'm sure even greater things are in store for you.

Love,
Your Mom

As you can imagine, Mrs. Jensen had a tough time getting through the letter without giving into tears. Other Family Scribe Groups tell me that they rarely make it through future-letter writing without passing a box of tissues around the reading circle.

Here are two other examples of letters. The first is from Carlos August and Angelica Marisol Esquival for their two children, Oliver and Andrea. Their letter, poetic and heartfelt, really captures these parents' love and confidence in their children. It appears in our second anthology in both Spanish and English:

Dedicatoria a los tesoros de nuestros corazones
Para nuestros hijos, Oliver y Andrea,
Sabemos que han pasado los años y que ustedes han estado creciendo como

dos capullitos de flor a los que vuestro padre y yo hemos cuidado con todo nuestro amor, cuidado y amorosa dedicación.

Poco a poco están abriendo sus pétalos a la vida, una vida linda y brillante que les espera adelante pero ante todo una vida bendecida por Dios en la cual su papá y yo confiamos que nos hagan felices y orgullosos con sus victorias alcanzadas y sean creadores de su propia felicidad y paz.

Los amamos con todo nuestro Corazón, y queremos que simpre lo tengan presente porque siempre serán para nosotros nuestros preciosos y adorados hijos, y que Dios me los bendiga hoy, mañana y siempre.

Sus Papás, Carlos Augusto y Angélica Marisol Esquival

(Dedicated to the treasures of our hearts
For our children, Oliver and Andrea,

We know that the years have passed and that you have grown like two flowers that your father and I have taken care of with all of our hearts, with careful and loving dedication.

Little by little you are opening your petals to life, a life beautiful and brilliant that awaits you, a life blessed by God in which your father and I are confident that you will make us happy and proud with your victories and that you will be creators of your own happiness and peace.

We love you with all of our hearts, and we want to always have you close, our precious and adorable children that God has given us for today, tomorrow and always.

Your parents, Carlos August and Angelica Marisol Esquival)

I have to repeat the obvious, which is that writing and reading these letters deeply affects the families. Other Family Writing Projects, in Las Vegas and across the country, have tried future-letter writing. Facilitators of those groups have told me that families in their groups have said future-letter writing was their favorite activity because of the powerful emotions and thoughts it summons. Families say that they will always remember writing and sharing the letters.

Friendship Notes

We have come a long way since the first day when we shared our artifacts and most of us were strangers. The artifacts provided small openings into our identities as individuals. With each week, however, our families have grown closer. They have gotten to know things about each other, sharing childhood memories, favorite foods, and hopes for the future.

Over time, the group has become a community. It is important that we reflect on how we have influenced each other. To do that, we continue with one last writing activity, one that flows nicely from future-letter writing. We write thank-you notes, with everyone writing at least four or five personal notes.

Before beginning this activity, we ask that everyone wait until all the notes have been written and delivered before beginning to read their stacks of mail. My partner and I have already written our thank-you notes, one from the two of us to every single person in the room. While the families are writing, we pass out our notes. Then we deliver the notes as parents and kids finish them.

When everyone is ready, we take time to silently read the notes. Not surprisingly, more than a few in the room quickly write responses and deliver them to their admirers. There are also lots of verbal exchanges and many blushes and smiles.

No one leaves the thank-you notes behind or drops them in the trash. Parents and students have told me that they saved thank-you mail from past years and still look at it from time to time.

Wrap-up

Look at the clock. Any time left? If so, initiate a discussion about your Family Scribe Group. Do families have comments or suggestions having to do with the way you facilitated? Are there ideas for changing or improving activities? Take the opportunity to let the families know that you will lead another Family Scribe Group and when it will meet. Solicit ideas for the next session, and find out which families think they will continue. Let those families know that you will stay in touch with them and that you welcome their suggestions. Use them as a base to build upon for future years.

In the weeks that have passed since the first meeting, we have brainstormed, scribed, and written poetry about our lives. We have looked at our surrounding community and defined our places in it. We have collected memories and shared childhoods. We have shared photographs of what matters to us and come to conclusions about what they portray about us. We have laughed, cried, and written together. We are a community. Our culminating activities, which are described in the next chapter, give us a chance to showcase our new community of family writers while also giving back to the community we call home.

8 Culminating Activities

The five weeks of writing and sharing have come to an end. Now what? It is time for a culminating activity or project. This activity does not necessarily center on writing. Its main objective is to involve the microcosm of the Family Scribe Group within the macrocosm of the surrounding community. Your group might contribute to its host school, community center, or church. Or it might focus on impacting your neighborhood or city. Possibly, the culminating activity will in some way publicize your Family Scribe Group by sharing your writings with others and bringing attention to your accomplishments. In this chapter, I discuss a few popular culminating activities in detail and also provide a long list of others.

Start thinking about your culminating activity ahead of time, possibly touching on it with your families at your first few meetings. They will undoubtedly have good ideas for you to consider as you shape your plans, and involving them in the planning process will make the activity their own. Look over the ideas in this chapter, and compile a list of activities that would work well at your site. You might schedule an additional meeting only for culminating activity planning or implementation. Our Fremont Scribes have used a sixth meeting for exactly those purposes, revising and editing pieces in the school's computer lab for our anthology or working in the garden or on a group mural. When you settle on a culminating activity, talk it through.

Gardens

In 2001, the Fremont Family Scribe Group chose to plant a community garden on the campus of our middle school. The project was a big undertaking and was funded largely by a Youth Neighborhood Association Partnership Program grant from the City of Las Vegas. In that first year, we spent close to $1,500 on gardening supplies and plants. All of our families, including some grandparents who had never before joined the group, showed up on campus one afternoon to plant hundreds of flowers and other plants in two gardens in our campus' central quad area. The garden project was significant for a number of reasons.

The gardens have gone a long way towards beautifying the school. John C. Fremont Middle School has not benefited from the sorts of landscaping and design that newer Clark County middle schools proudly boast. Before we began our garden project, the campus looked extremely bland, with light blue walls of peeling paint surrounding the quad. There was little landscaping other than an empty grassy area surrounded by asphalt and concrete. Our two gardens changed all of that by adding a splash of color and bringing a sense of vitality to an otherwise bleak setting.

We have continued with the community gardens since that time, adding new plants to the primary garden in the quad area each year at the beginning and end of our group. In the Fremont Family Scribe Group's third year, we added a selection of native cacti in front of the school in an area that the school district had promised to landscape when the school was renovated at the end of the 1990s. For two or three years the area sat empty except for trash that blew against the school. Now, after the cacti have had some time to grow, the native plant garden adds greatly to the school's appearance from the street. The native plants, we feel, represent our members as a collection of natives and transplants to Las Vegas, working to survive in the desert.

Besides the obvious aesthetic reasons for planting the gardens, the flowers, bushes, and cacti we have set into the earth symbolize the putting down of roots our families have achieved during our project. Many of the parents have never before felt a part of the school community. Language barriers have kept some from feeling comfortable at the school. Others have only been called to campus for conferences with counselors or deans when there have been problems with their children at school. Some have just never felt they had a place on the campus or a concrete reason to be there—school was for their kids. These attitudes changed during the Family Scribe Group, when parents not only found they had a place at the school but also a hand in creating that place.

Putting down roots is also important for children. A school like ours, at the heart of a fast-growing city, experiences an extremely high rate of student transience. Students come and go from the school on a daily basis. The student who begins and ends middle-school life at John C. Fremont is the exception. Planting the garden gave the students a chance to have a spot at school that was their own, that reflected not only their efforts but also their very presence at the school. In fact, it was a Family Scribe Group student, Erendira, who really took it upon herself to care for the garden two or three days a week after school the year it was planted. Erendira and her parents moved away from our neighborhood before her eighth-grade year and we lost contact with her after the move. Still, I see some of her passion and care reflected in the garden every time I see it in bloom.

Another reason for the garden, which ties in very closely with the idea of putting down roots, was that by working the soil and planting roses, bush daisies, and other plants that would survive for years to come, the families were gaining a real sense of ownership and empowerment at the school. Now the campus became theirs. Their positive and lasting mark on the landscape speaks to their presence at school.

Murals

In the second and fourth years of the Fremont Family Scribe Group, we continued to work on the gardens but also turned our efforts in another direction. We had brought color to the quad area with our plants. Now we turned to the outer walls of the school, which are rarely, if ever, cleaned or painted by the district. Truthfully, cleaning the walls would quite likely cause paint to fall off, making a bad situation worse. Not having the resources to paint the entire school, we decided instead to create a Family Scribe Group mural across from the garden in the quad area that faces the school's main entrance.

For the theme of the mural, we looked to the families themselves. Two of the most important traits that jumped out at us from the families were their diversity and sense of joy. Our group was diverse with regards to language, culture, ethnicity, and family grouping. The mural had to capture those elements, which we realized represented the school community as a whole. Joy jumped off the pages of our group's writings—joy with family, heritage, and achievements—so we wanted our mural to jump off the wall of the school with an equal sense of joy.

To capture these traits, we designed a mural with eight human figures of various sizes jumping into the air, some holding hands, others with their arms raised. Our models for the mural were children from the project, except one tall adult at the center, who, I have to confess, is me. To represent the diversity of our group, we painted the human silhouettes each a different color. A blue figure leaps into the arms of a yellow being who waves at a green person across the way. The mural works. It captures the essence of our project and accomplishes the same goals as our garden by beautifying the campus and leaving our collective mark upon it. But what about writing?

We incorporated writing into the mural by painting 150 ceramic tiles with phrases and images that we thought captured the spirit of our writing group. One tile depicts a green foreground spotted with colorful flowers and the word "Felicidad" shining through a rainbow. Another reads "Friends for Life" in red, green, and orange letters that are surrounded by hearts. They are to the point. One says simply "WRITE" in bold letters and the other, "COMMUNITY."

The mural remains the colorful focal point of our school's campus and has become an ongoing project for the families. Our fall 2003 group picked up where the spring 2002 group left off by painting another 80 tiles for the mural. One student, Carlos Oliver Esquival, wrote, "Our mural is growing like a tree that someday might cover the entire campus, bringing our happiness and creativity to the whole school." He might be right. Each succeeding year we add a few more tiles.

These culminating activities of the Fremont Family Scribe Group aimed to benefit the school as a whole while at the same time empowering the families as members of that community. Two other culminating projects that the Fremont Family Scribe Group has undertaken have had different goals. It is important to us that people from outside our immediate community have the chance to hear and see our work. Publishing is an important and integral element of every Family Scribe Group. Usually, publishing takes the form of a group anthology that includes a cross-section of writings from a group, with photos and artwork. In 2003 and 2004, we turned our publishing efforts in other directions.

Audio Projects

As part of a City of Las Vegas neighborhood grant in 2003, we purchased some recording equipment that we used to capture our family members reading poems, stories, and short essays that they had written. Then we used grant money from a community park center in our school's neighborhood to purchase blank CDs and the software to design a CD cover. From the school district we borrowed a high-speed CD copying device that was able to burn several hundred CDs overnight. The result: *Family Matters*, a spoken-word CD that features every one of our spring 2003 Fremont Family Scribe Group members reading something that they wrote while in the group. Thematically, the CD deals with family members' thoughts about the group itself, their heritages, their lives in the here and now of Las Vegas, and their hopes and dreams for the future.

The CD gives us something to share with others. It's formatted to fit a thirty-minute slot on the radio, and it is our hope that we will be able to have it featured on local public radio or some other family-friendly, community-oriented station. Also, the families can share the CD with relatives and friends. I expect that, years from now, kids from our project who have grown up will pull out the CD to show their own children.

Websites

Another culminating activity of the Fremont Family Scribe Group, one which will undoubtedly continue over the next few years, is the creation of a Family Scribe Group website, www.FamilyWritingProjects.com. Our spring 2004 group met in the school's computer lab to put much of their writing into files that could be transferred easily to the Web. The website has expanded to include many other Family Scribe Groups, some from across the country and others from right here in Las Vegas.

Like the spoken-word CD *Family Matters*, the website is a way to publish writing. The Fremont Family Scribe Group previously had claimed ground on the school campus through gardens and murals, symbolizing the group's presence as stakeholders and community members. Now, on the Internet, the Fremont Family Scribe Group shows itself to be a leader in family writing and marks its place as a pioneer within the Family Scribe Group network across the nation.

Culminating activities have played an extremely important role in the definition of the Fremont Family Scribe Group. They have given our families a chance to benefit our school and to draw attention to themselves. There are many culminating activities a Family Scribe Group can undertake besides gardens, murals, CDs, and websites that will meet these same goals in different ways.

The remainder of this chapter suggests twenty-five possible culminating activities, listed alphabetically, that a Family Scribe Group might want to undertake once the writing is done. Some suggestions are large, others small. Look around your site and decide what is needed and what you can do. It may be that paint is peeling on school benches or playground equipment is wearing out. You may see opportunities to publicize your project while at the same time enriching your community. Once you have decided what is needed, discuss what your Family Scribe Group will have to do to meet your goals. What will be done and who will do it? The following ideas are a starting point for generating possible culminating activities.

Culminating Activities

Anthology. A final anthology is an important artifact that marks a group's hard work. Make plenty of extra copies to share with school district administrators and local civic/political leaders and to keep for future groups.

Calendar. This publishes work and is also a possible fundraiser. Design a calendar with photos, poems, and quotes. The calendar makes a practical keepsake for group members. Extra copies bring in money and expand your outreach.

Campus beautification. Look at your site and see what you can do to make it a little better for everyone who spends time there. Paint benches, pull weeds, get gum up off the sidewalk. Lots of little changes will make a big difference. Write about your planned improvements and then reflect afterwards with poetry or essays.

CD-ROM or DVD. If your group includes members who are technologically inclined, you might consider creating a CD-ROM or DVD with audio and video from your group. Include clips from actual meetings and recordings of writers reading their pieces. Is there a local TV or public radio station or other community-oriented station that will play your work?

Cleanup day. Get families together for some neighborhood cleanup. Check with neighbors ahead of time to see if there are some who could use help weeding their yards or picking up branches. Write thank-you notes to the people who let you help them.

Clothing drive. Collect and wash secondhand clothes and donate them to a local agency that works with needy families in your community. Everyone can write about how they feel when they help others. Or write a narrative about the clothes that were donated. Maybe a t-shirt or dress has a story behind it.

Community garden. This is one of the best projects to undertake because of the benefits to the community. A flower garden will bring color to your site; vegetables bring flavor. Plant a garden where others will watch it grow and bloom. It can be small, planted in flowerpots or planters outside your school or church. You might think big and cultivate a spot that you will keep growing for years to come as an ongoing undertaking of Family Scribe Groups.

Cookbook. Food and family projects go hand-in-hand. In the cookbook collect family recipes, traditional recipes, and recipes from potlucks. Add family stories or write poems about the foods. As with the calendar, group members will treasure the cookbook for years to come and will refer to it, not only for recipes but also as a memory of the group. Cookbooks are a great fundraising item and a clever way to publish writing.

Display board. Create a display board and post photos and writings that celebrate the group's writing. Find a busy location in your community, such as a bank lobby or a school office, in which to place the display board.

Family field trip. Pick a place to visit and write about. After five weeks of writing indoors, find a park, lake, or mountain to inspire new ideas for writing. Visit a local history museum and write poems or stories based on what you learned. Write a ballad about your town or a fictional tale about how your city was founded. Publish the works as a literature-of-place anthology.

Flowerpots. Get crafty with flowerpots. Decorate them with paint, glitter, and whatever else you can find. Adorn them with poems and words that capture your group. Create a garden with the painted pots, or sell them as a fundraiser. Fill the community with your words and flowers.

Food drive. If you have a fall Family Scribe Group, plan ahead to finish your group with a holiday food drive. Donate canned goods to a shelter or check with local agencies to see if they can recommend a family to adopt. Include letters of appreciation with your collection of foods.

Graffiti cleanup. Is graffiti a problem at your site or in your community? Get permission from the owner of a wall or sign to whitewash away the problem. Or replace those illiterate tags with something literate of your own, with the owner's permission.

Hospital or nursing home visit. Redecorate a recreation room or TV room at a local hospital or nursing home. Spruce up a hospital waiting room with books of poetry, a few houseplants, and colorful posters or paintings. Perhaps members can hang framed poems they have written as part of the decorations.

Interviews. Go into the community to collect stories of longtime locals. Put together an anthology of their tales. Interview them about their recollections of how things used to be. See if they can come up with unique photographs or other relics that capture the community's past.

Letters abroad. Find out the names of people from your community serving overseas in the armed forces. Regularly write letters to them filled with information about what is going on back home.

Mural. A mural is a lasting representation of your group. The possibilities are unlimited. Come up with a design that contains elements important to the families in your group. Incorporate writing with your artwork.

Open-mic night. Host an open-mic night at which local writers can read their works. Invite students from local schools, and offer prizes to those who participate.

Poetry board. Look for community bulletin boards at grocery stores, gas stations, schools, churches, shopping malls, and other places where people come and go. Get permission to post a poem or two at a time. The poems will catch people's attention and advertise your group.

Public performance. Is there a place in the community where you can give a public reading? Read work in a public library or at a local festival. Check with your school and other community organizations about upcoming meetings at which your group can read a number of pieces.

Tree planting. Plant native plants: pines in the Rocky Mountain States, cacti in the Southwest, sunflowers in Kansas. Put down roots, beautify your neighborhood, and then write about the experience.

T-shirts. Design t-shirts that represent your group. Print a group poem on the front or back, or list golden lines uttered during class by participants. Create a design that links symbolically with your work. See if you can raise funds for your group by selling shirts to families, faculty members, and neighbors.

Website. Set up a website with writing, photos, and other artifacts. Link your site to FamilyWritingProjects.com, or send your files to the website and we will add your group to our growing assemblage of webpages. Publicize your web presence in a community newsletter. Share yourselves with the world.

Welcome center. Create a welcome center with information about your school or site. Make a list of things people new to your location should know. Write about them and collect them in a book that newcomers can read.

Write-a-thon. How long can your group put pen to paper? Solicit sponsors from the community, maybe for a penny per word or fifty cents a page. Take a day to write, write, and write. Use the donations for your next Family Scribe Group, or donate the pledges to a local charity.

Writers' night. Host a writers' night. Invite families to join you for an evening of writing activities. Share some of your group's work with the families, then involve them in a writing activity. Publish the finished works.

This list of ideas will give you plenty of workable ideas to use at your site—but you do not need to limit yourselves to the list. Involve the families in the decision-making process, and your culminating activity will succeed because of their enthusiasm.

9 Project Themes and Activities

In this chapter, I introduce possible themes and activities that a Family Scribe Group could adopt. The ideas, listed alphabetically, are only a few of the many that you can develop. I am certain that if you sit down with a pen and paper, you can come up with many of your own. However, thousands of combinations of themes and activities can be put together using only the ideas in this chapter.

Many of the activities would fit under more than one theme. In fact, it is possible to select a theme that you think would work well with your group and then search through the following activities to find several that will work with your theme. This list offers more practical ideas for activities than could possibly fit into a single Family Scribe Group—realistically, you'll need only a handful of activities. Alternatively, these activities could be shaped to fit with almost any theme you can think up for your families to use as their guiding idea. The list is by no means exhaustive—hopefully, while reading it, you will come up with some ideas of your own that you can undertake with your project. The trick is to think of activities that will lead naturally into some sort of writing.

Some of the activities listed in this section overlap with the culminating projects in the previous chapter. For example, Scribe Groups have designed calendars as a weekly activity, using the calendars as a jumping-off point for writing, while others have used calendars as culminating activities to showcase their Scribe Group. How you choose to use these ideas is up to you and your families.

Themes and Activities

American life. This is a theme that several parents have told me would make a great subject for a group. The question of what it means to be an American has many answers. Different families will undoubtedly have different ways of interpreting their American-ness. This theme generates understanding and bridges cultures.

Artifact sharing. This kick-off activity from the Fremont Family Scribe Group leads to creating a group poem and is important enough to list again here. The artifact sharing gives everyone an opportunity to meet the rest of the group. It also gives each person an equal chance, right from the beginning, to be heard.

Authors' night. Family Scribe Group members could plan an authors' night at their site. Family members could read their works and possibly lead the audience in a writing activity. Also, a guest author could attend and share ideas about writing and some of his or her works.

Autobiography. Everyone has a story to tell. With this theme, parents would have the welcome opportunity to write about events in their lives, while children are enabled to put their childhoods into words.

Bookmaking. Allow everyone to make his or her own book filled with artwork, poems, stories, and other writing. Along the way, participants might share books they have read and names of authors who have affected their lives.

Celebrating diversity. One of the most frequent comments of parents and children in the Fremont Family Scribe Group is that the group gives them a chance to learn from people who are different from them. This theme will provide opportunities to increase understanding and empathy among families of diverse backgrounds.

Ceramic tiles. In our second year of the Fremont Family Scribe Group, we worked with our school's art teacher to design a mural using four-inch ceramic tiles. We painted the tiles with words and images drawn from our project and writings. Then we arranged the tiles on a wall around a life-size painting of human figures embracing and leaping. The mural is a centerpiece of our school as well a public display of our work. You might use the tiles in a mural or let everyone take theirs home as souvenirs.

Changing places. Your school population may be transient. Perhaps new populations are entering your area. This theme gives the opportunity for families to write about the changes their lives are undergoing in the move from one place to another.

Child's point-of-view. This theme invites parents to look at life from the points-of-view of their children and gives kids a chance to explain how they view the world. Parents often love the chance to remember how they viewed life as a child and put those memories into writing.

Creative artist. This theme explores music, artwork, dance, or any other art form that families find important. Families share and create artistic projects that lead to writing opportunities. Or they might investigate art forms they know little about.

Cultural interchange. In a school or community with many international families, or with families of diverse backgrounds, this theme encourages families to interact and share cultural ideas and traditions.

Diary or journal writing. This activity would work with any theme you choose. Families members could keep individual journals or share a journal at home. Dialogue journals between families also would be an exciting activity—this might be especially important in a project themed around multicultural awareness or family traditions.

Dreams and hopes. Again and again, this topic comes up during Family Scribe Groups. A group with this theme looks at both nighttime dreams and daydreams as well as the hopes families hold for themselves.

Family books. In projects that adopt a theme centering on the family or genealogy, the making of family books would certainly be exciting. Each family could work on creating a book about themselves, including photos, artwork, stories, quotes, poetry, newspaper articles, and anything else they find important. Scrapbooking has become extremely popular in recent years, and lots of creative materials are available for making personal scrapbooks.

Family culture and traditions. This theme takes a cultural anthropologist's perspective on families. Together, parents and children discuss and write about both their common and unique lifestyles and their own particular folklores. This theme brings out similarities between families, while giving them a chance to celebrate their cultural differences. Holidays, family gatherings, and special family traditions become the focus of the group.

Family flags or crests. Each family could work to design a flag or crest with images representing their lives. Then, they could write about their designs and how the images reflect aspects of their family.

Family matters. What makes a family important? What makes families work? These issues form the theme of a project focusing exclusively on the family itself.

Family role-playing. Family members can act out various role-plays, then write about their thoughts or feelings about the role-playing. For example, the parents could act like their children, while the kids get to play to the roles of their parents.

Food. We have used a potluck lunch as an activity in the Fremont Family Scribe Group. The Fitzgerald Family Scribe Group in Las Vegas facilitated a wonderful project with the title "Cooking in Mama's Kitchen." They invited everyone to share food, create recipe poems about their families, and write about memories having to do with food.

Gardens. This theme considers gardens, both physically and metaphorically. Families work together on a gardening project, while considering their own lives, roots, and growth.

Genealogy. Family histories, ancestry, and ethnic heritage, as well as how the past leads to our present and future lives, are components of genealogy that will shape an exciting Family Scribe Group. Children exploring this theme learn about their family's past, while parents have the opportunity to discuss and write about relatives and stories their children might not know about.

Hobbies. This theme gives everyone time to share their hobbies, write about what interests them, and learn what others do in their free time.

Journeys. Life is a journey, but so is a summer vacation. The theme of journeys leads families to look at the journeys they have already embarked upon. It could also lend itself to families planning future journeys.

Letter writing. The Fremont Family Scribe Group has used future-letter writing as an activity in its final week with great success. Letter writing could take many forms: letters could be written to local community leaders in a social-action-themed project, to distant family members in a family-themed project, or to pen pals in a cultural-exchange-themed project. Really, letter writing could find a place in nearly any Family Scribe Group you undertake.

Local history. No city, town, or rural setting is devoid of local lore. By taking local history as a theme, a family group collects stories or lets members share their family histories.

Magnets. The Rex Bell Family Scribe Group in Las Vegas designed refrigerator magnets that everyone could keep as souvenirs of their time together. Of course, they wrote about their magnet designs!

Mapmaking. The Fremont Family Scribe Group's members have made maps of their childhood settings and then used those to explore how those settings shape their identity. Maps and the writing they inspire will fit well into projects with themes such as childhood point-of-view, cultural interchange, local history, and oral traditions.

Music. Music stirs everyone's emotions. This theme leads group members to listen to familiar and not-so-familiar musical styles and artists. Members can write reviews of music they particularly like or write and play their own music.

Natural environment. In Las Vegas, the desert Southwest makes a fascinating theme. So does the environment in which you teach and live. Families consider how the environment affects their lives. They write about city life, life in rural settings, or about the different environments in which they have lived over the course of time.

Newspaper or newsletter. A Family Scribe Group could incorporate all of its work into a newspaper or newsletter for distribution around their school or community. They could also sell their product as a way of raising funds.

Oral traditions. Oral traditions preserve the past but always face the threat of being lost along the way. Families in a group exploring this theme would use writing to preserve and share stories from their families and community.

Our school. Here, the theme is the school, community center, church, or other organization sponsoring the group. Family members explore aspects of their site that they like or dislike, and they make suggestions for improvement. Or they might research its history and put together an anthology that celebrates the site's story.

Photography and photographs. Most families have albums of photos. Nearly everyone likes to take photos and share them. This theme immerses participants in photographs of ancestors and relatives, as well as pictures they have already taken of their families. It also leads to activities involving taking pictures during the duration of the Family Scribe Group. We have also used photography in our own project, capturing images around where we live. Photography would work great in a project studying the natural environment. Everyone can take photos around their school or immediate community as a prompt for social action or a project dealing specifically with their town or community.

Picture frames. If you use photography in your project, you might consider an activity in which everyone decorates a picture frame with paint, beads, glitter, or other objects.

Puzzle making. Family members might make puzzles about their own lives. Or they could make puzzles about their surrounding community. These might be simple crossword puzzles or word searches, or writers could come up with riddles that tie in with the project's theme. Perhaps the entire group could design a puzzle with parts representing the various families.

Quilts. Quilts could be made of artwork, poems, photos, or just about anything else your group finds important. The quilt can then be displayed at your site or publicly at a local business.

Role models. Participants think about who the important people are in their lives. They might be world or national figures but could also be family members or friends. Writers define what it means to be a role model and decide how they can become role models to others.

Sculpture garden. Participants might first design sculptures, then arrange them in an area where others will see them. As with the mural and garden projects, a sculpture garden will empower members by giving them a physical stake in your site's appearance.

Social action. This theme gives families an opportunity to identify an issue or problem in their community that concerns them. They discuss and write about the issue and formulate some sort of action they can take to work on solving the matter. This can lead to writing letters to the editor or working directly in the community in some way.

Storytelling. Stories from books, relatives, and participants' own lives provide more than enough material for a Family Scribe Group using this theme. I am sure that young children would love this theme, but it works just as well with older students and their parents.

Video. The entire Family Scribe Group could make a video that everyone could keep and which could be shown publicly. The video might include scenes from group meetings and showcase members reading their work, or it might document a culminating activity from the planning stages to completion.

Word Processing. Schedule a day in the computer lab so that everyone has a chance to edit and revise his/her work. It has been my experience that the children will lead the way, helping their parents put together final pieces with clip art and graphics.

Yearbook. The Silverado High School Family Scribe Group in Las Vegas created a yearbook for ESL Students. The yearbook was written in a number of languages and included information that students new to this country would find valuable.

10 Benefits of Family Scribe Groups

*F*acilitators who design and lead Family Scribe Groups witness a broad range of benefits, not only for the community of family writers with whom they work but also for themselves. This chapter outlines these benefits and outcomes as they affect facilitators and families. Keep all of these ideas in mind when developing and leading a Family Scribe Group. Many of them will come naturally; others may need conscious attention. You will find that in following this approach to facilitating, not only will your project succeed, but you will find yourself becoming a stronger teacher.

Affirmation. For teachers and others working within school systems (and other educational settings) that have the potential to depersonalize education, Scribe Groups are reaffirming experiences. Many teachers begin their careers with dreams of making an impact on the lives of others, only to later feel alienated by curriculum needs, testing demands, supervisor controls, or student apathy and disinterest. These conditions too often breed cynicism and aloofness to what matters in students' lives. The intimacy and relevance that so greatly define Scribe Groups may not only ward off such attitudes in teachers but can go a long way toward dissolving cynicism and burn-out. Teachers leading Scribe Groups see that they make a difference and feel as if there is a need and appreciation for their work. This little haven, where so much sharing, talking, and writing takes place—and where kids and families want to be in their free time—becomes a place of renewal and optimism.

Insight into families and students. Teachers who take on the challenge of working with families gain critical and lasting insight into their students and their students' lives and families. This insight is in no way an intrusion or violation of privacy. Rather, it is a sharing of ideas and emotions that takes place on equal footing. Too often, the only time teachers, particularly in middle and high school, have the opportunity to meet parents is when a student is in trouble at school or doing poorly on class work. Under those circumstances, contact with families rarely yields meaningful understanding and all too often turns into blame sessions aimed at students or even their parents.

In a Scribe Group, the things that are important to families are explored, common values and needs are expressed, and the teacher and family transform into members of equal standing in the community. The doors of communication between teachers and families, as well as within families themselves, are opened. Families in Scribe Groups get to know their children's teachers in new and important ways. As a result, parents feel more comfortable at school and gain insight into how teachers work with their children. This dynamic seems to be especially true for families who might already feel marginalized, such as those with students in special education classes, English as a Second Language programs, or those who come from ethnic or language minority groups. In a Family Scribe Group, these families are at the center of learning, rather than on the outside looking in.

Autonomy and ownership. Autonomy and ownership are rare in education. In a Scribe Group, a teacher can find a place to teach that lies outside of daily educational restraints. The themes a Scribe Group explores, the activities it undertakes, and the goals it achieves are all its own. It is an excellent opportunity to take part in the creation of something rare and beautiful: an autonomous group of interested and driven writers. The families also gain a sense of ownership by becoming shareholders in the entire workings of a Scribe Group. Rather than watching as outsiders to the educational process, parents work alongside their children and the facilitator. The kids' energy and ideas are driving forces just as much as the facilitator's are.

Community. A Family Scribe Group develops a strong sense of community. For teachers, who frequently commute to work, the Scribe Group might represent the first time they feel genuinely involved in the communities where they teach. Similarly, for families who live in urban settings or in neighborhoods with high levels of diversity, a Scribe Group might be the one opportunity they have to come together to share and work on common interests.

Grade levels, departments, languages, and other subdivisions often fragment schools. A Scribe Group brings together members of various groups within a school to create a cohesive community. This community sense is especially important because it contributes directly to the writing: trust is an important element of any Scribe Group. Members must feel valued if they are going to share ideas and stories that are often personal and revealing. The Family Scribe Group community generates these elements of value and trust.

A sense of accomplishment. Facilitators of Scribe Groups gain a strong and valid sense of accomplishment. They recognize that they have had a large part in creating something new at their school, community center, or church. Not only have these facilitators brought together parents with their kids to share experiences, discuss ideas, and write it all down, but they have also created a sense of community between families that might otherwise have never known or understood each other. Facilitators, as well as parents and kids, gain the sense that, in a small way, they are changing things by writing together. The changes might appear small at first, affecting only a school or a neighborhood. But there is a sense among Scribe Group members that they are planting seeds for the future in ways that, for now, can only be guessed at.

Creativity. Creative ideas and creative impulses thrive in Family Scribe Groups. For facilitators this is especially important, as it gives them the chance to try out new ideas, explore themes, and experiment with possibilities. Facilitators who also teach in public schools remark how wonderful it is to create freely and to work with an enthused group of writers. They see that the issues that are most important to families are issues overlooked almost entirely by schools. For families in projects, creativity is at the center of their experience. Very often, parents and kids in Scribe Groups remark that their group is an island, a place where they can work creatively and cooperatively together. For them, the Scribe Group becomes a break from the demands of their everyday realities.

The opportunity to give back. Working with families at a school, church, or other neighborhood location is a way of giving back to the community. For facilitators, there is the sense of having done something for others simply for the good of doing it.

In a Scribe Group, facilitators have the chance to give time, that valuable and elusive commodity, to members of the community where they teach. Of course, good teachers will always acknowledge how much they gain from their students. But a Scribe Group is a chance to reciprocate, not only to students but to their families as well. For families, the project is an opportunity to give something to their school or community site. This is especially true when families publish their work and undertake a community-oriented culminating activity, one that benefits their school, neighborhood, or community.

Relevance. Family Scribe Groups do not deal in formulaic writing or stale exercises. They do not teach what others have decided is important to learn or what benchmarks or curriculum guides list as important. Instead, the work of Scribe Groups is relevant and real—it is families writing about themselves. For the facilitator this has enormous implications. It means that the writers with whom they are working respond from an intrinsic sense of motivation. They are writing about what they know best and what they want to write about. Far too often teachers complain about being unable to motivate students to write. But in a Scribe Group, it seems there is too much going on not to write! The urge to write will sweep up even reluctant writers.

Growth as a classroom teacher. Scribe Group facilitators who also teach take some of what they have learned working with families back into their classrooms and apply it in their teaching and interactions with students. The broadened understanding of students' lives outside of school and of their families' personalities will change how a teacher views all of his or her students in class. The successes of relevant writing themes and topics in a Scribe Group will lead a classroom teacher to strive for relevance and meaning. The successes of reluctant writers in Scribe Groups remind a teacher to find ways of motivating similarly reluctant writers in class instead of taking an "Oh, well" attitude towards their hesitation. When back in the classroom, a group facilitator should feel empowered and confident and be more inclined to take writing risks with students.

Energy and enthusiasm. Family Scribe Groups take a lot of effort. But, like a good workout that leaves an exerciser feeling ecstatic on endorphins, the work of a Scribe Group energizes facilitators. Rather than feeling depleted or worn out, facilitators feel like they have gained strength and inspiration. Why? Facilitating a Family Scribe Group has affirmed their desire to teach and work with students. It has generated a sense of autonomy and ownership, validating their work. Along the way they have gained insight into their students' families and taken part in the creation of a new community of writers. Their work has been creative, leaving a strong sense of accomplishment. Facilitators can see that they have given valuable gifts back to their communities, not the least of which is an appreciation for the importance of relevant writing in our lives.

All of these factors invariably leave facilitators and the families with whom they work feeling inspired and charged up. How often do both teachers and students reach the end of a semester or course feeling as though they could not have taken one more class session? All the time. The scenario is extremely different with Scribe Groups. Before projects end, families begin asking about the next project. Ideas generated in one project lead to the desire to continue on as writers. Facilitators come to the end of a Scribe Group and invariably have arrived at their own conclusions about how to do a better job next time or about themes or activities they want to try out. It is rare for facilitators not to want to continue.

Facilitators' Resources

Benefits for Administrators

*F*amily Scribe Groups benefit both teachers and administrators. As you read, ask yourself if the benefits I've described apply to you and your situation. This section is particularly useful for administrators who may be hesitant to try a Scribe Group on their campuses.

Reasons to Start Family Scribe Groups

To develop strong school–home connections. This applies regardless of the location of the school but is especially important in urban settings and in secondary schools where teachers can struggle to connect with parents. Too often, especially in middle and high school, the only times teachers and parents meet are when there are problems concerning their children to sort out. Facilitators find that students who participate with their families in Scribe Groups tend to work harder in class and demonstrate more confidence as writers. Administrators recognize that parent involvement is crucial to their schools' successes. In fact, parent involvement is now often required at Title I schools and through the No Child Left Behind legislation. A Family Scribe Group creates direct connections between school and home, connections that are overwhelmingly positive and productive. This section is particularly useful for administrators who may be hesitant and offers the following reasons for starting a Family Scribe Group on their campuses.

To involve parents in schools. The Family Scribe Group is a rare opportunity for teachers to work with parents, to empower them, and to give them respect and a place in the school setting that is productive and creative. At the same time, a Scribe Group is a hands-on setting in which parents become leaders in their children's eyes. Parents often ask teachers how they can help their children or get them to do schoolwork at home. Scribe Groups are a non-threatening and encouraging setting in which parents are able to work alongside their children, modeling the attitudes and behaviors regarding school that they want to see in their children.

To create a school-based learning community. For both teachers and their administrators, one of the most exciting dimensions of a Family Scribe Group is the school-based learning community that grows naturally as the group develops. The Scribe Group becomes a microcosm of the larger school community. It opens lines of communication and enables diverse and often marginalized groups to become friends who work together. This community aspect also reaches out into the surrounding neighborhood and city as members write about their lives and share their works with others or undertake culminating projects that benefit their communities.

To provide a setting in which students become energetically involved at school. A Family Scribe Group is a focused and intense forum in which students become absorbed with what might otherwise be thought of as schoolwork. They voluntarily come to school on their own time to engage with others. Students in Family Scribe Groups really learn to appreciate their schools. They write about their schools, and they learn to view them as places where people come together to create. Facilitators almost always observe that students involved in Family Scribe Groups demonstrate more positive feelings about school than their peers. These kids feel as though they have a stake in the school. For administrators, this is a strong reason to see a group organized at their sites. They recognize that students in Scribe Groups develop pride and a sense of belonging in their school.

To create an atmosphere where writing flourishes. Here is an opportunity to translate an academic subject into real life. Our mantra is that the writing must be meaningful and relevant to the families. With that goal met, it is hard to stop the writing. Students and their families begin to see themselves as writers. They engage themselves with topics and find audiences for their work, both within the Scribe Group and in the greater school and neighborhood communities. Writing becomes fun and purposeful rather than a classroom drill. Student writers in Scribe Groups are not intimidated by writing situations that come up away from the Scribe Group, such as writing proficiency exams. They are writers and feel competent enough to excel on such measures of their writing skills.

To expand students' writing skills. In school, students study different writing genres and styles. In the Scribe Group, they apply those approaches to topics that they feel are important. Students in the Scribe Group really have an upper hand when it comes to writing. Both teachers and administrators can appreciate the growth students make as writers in a Scribe Group. Student writers in Scribe Groups will also take chances and write in ways that classroom writing never approaches. From these experiences, students really learn to appreciate the ways that writing connects with life.

To establish the writing process as a part of students', families', and teachers' lives. Life and family experiences are the center of Scribe Groups. All stages of the writing process, from prewriting to final drafts, come into play during a project's work. And they are firmly connected with the writers' lives. Of course, this fact motivates writers to express themselves clearly, with emotion and detail. Life too often gets in the way of writing, making it hard to find the time to express thoughts on paper. Frequently, facilitators who are teachers credit their involvement with the Scribe Group as the catalyst that reinserts writing into their own lives. Scribe Groups give teachers a time to write instead of just teaching others to write. This, in turn, causes them to elevate writing in importance and share that value with their projects' families and their school community. Coming to school to write about their lives becomes as important to facilitators as it does to the families. This dynamic creates a culture of literacy with an emphasis on writing that all administrators should readily appreciate at their sites.

To initiate a valuable and rewarding long-term project at school. The field of education is constantly overrun with fads and programs that do not last. Teachers and administrators alike are often exasperated by a seemingly endless barrage of new programs or teaching techniques that fade quickly only to be replaced by another.

For a successful Family Scribe Group, the situation is quite different. A Family Scribe Group grows and adapts organically to the needs and interests of families, teachers, and their schools. The families and teachers themselves determine the work of a Scribe Group. Scribe Groups never really seem to end. The work of each project at a site builds upon previous projects, creating a continuous thread of involvement. Students and families want to be involved, creating a situation in which teachers are able to maintain continuity and expand their project's goals as time goes by.

To showcase the talents and ideas of students, teachers, and families. This project may be a school's best opportunity to pool resources to provide visibility for the school in the community. Anthologies, murals, gardens, clothing or food drives, and websites are all current examples of ways that Family Scribe Groups display their talents and efforts. These all reflect positively on schools, administrators, teachers, families, and students.

To facilitate understanding. Understanding of others arises in many ways during a Family Scribe Group's time together. Teachers learn about their students' lives and the lives of their students' families. Facilitators regularly remark that this aspect of the Family Scribe Group is the most rewarding and exciting one for them. They find that these increased levels of understanding change how they view their students at school and how they teach in the classroom. Similarly, students and their families find out that their teachers are real people with lives away from the school. They grow to appreciate them as individuals, and they gain insight into what motivates them to be teachers.

Administrators realize that this bridge between families and teachers strengthens their schools. Parents who believe in their children's teachers are supporters of the schools they attend and are often more willing to become involved in other school interests, such as serving on committees or volunteering to help with school needs.

To step out of restrictive roles. Teachers love the freedom they experience as Scribe Group facilitators. No longer are they teachers who stand up in front and lead while everyone else does the work. Facilitators write alongside families. They do the same activities as their students. In the process, they learn about themselves, their own families, and their communities just as the family participants do. Teachers find this process liberating and energizing.

I have seen a few administrators participate alongside families in Scribe Groups. I believe it is important that more administrators join projects. Undoubtedly, they find that giving up a little bit of control brings rewards of its own. Similarly, administrators observing Scribe Groups working on their campuses see that their teachers are working alongside families in ways that previously had not existed. This partnership strengthens schools while benefiting everyone involved.

Sample Project

*I*n this next section, I construct a sample five-week Family Scribe Group using several of the activities described in **Chapters 8 and 9**. The theme for the project will be "Family Matters." The hypothetical project will meet five times, for around two hours each time. A final sixth meeting, at which everyone will have a chance to edit and revise their writings, as well as create a final project, follows the five weeks of class.

Week One

- Sign-in
- Artifact sharing
- Group poem
- Family flags (part one)

For Week One, include the request with invitations that each family brings several items they think represent their family. For instance, someone might bring a cookbook because he or she loves to cook for the family. Another person might bring keys to the car because the family car is used like a taxi to shuffle everyone around to their various activities.

After each person has had a chance to share, let everyone reflect in their journals about what they chose to bring and what they saw others share. Then let everyone who wants to read aloud have the chance to discuss the ideas that artifact sharing inspired. Each individual then selects several images, words, or phrases from their writing. Combine these to create a group poem that includes some contribution from each person in the group.

Now everyone is thinking about their own families as well as aspects of the other families in their new writing group. Ask everyone to list half a dozen or more objects or ideas that they think strongly represent their own family. Share these lists aloud.

The lists are really brainstorms for creating family flags. Tell the families that next week they will create flags or banners that represent their own families. As a homework assignment, they can collect small items or pictures to put on the flags. If they do not actually bring things to put on their flags, let them know that you will have various art supplies such as glitter glue, beads, watercolors, markers, and colored pencils.

Week Two

- Sign-in
- Family flags (part two)
- Writing about flags
- Presenting flags and reading aloud

Begin class by reviewing the group poem from Week One. Invite anyone who wishes to share the family lists that they wrote in Week One to read again as a way of reminding everyone about the task at hand, creating family flags. For the next hour or so, let families experiment with the supplies you provide. Undoubtedly, many of the flags will display common themes. It is just as certain that individual families will include images or words specific to their own lives. As families finish with their designs, they can begin writing in their journals. On the overhead projector or chalkboard, have a prompt, such as one or all of the following:

> What do you think your flag says about your family?
> Which words or images seem most important to you?
> Explain the overall theme of your flag.

Once the flags are made and the writings finished, hang the flags from yarn or twine across the room or tack them to the wall. Let each family have a few minutes to show off their work and read from their journals.

Follow up the sharing and reading with a group discussion of how the different flags combine to make a community, just as our many state flags make up the whole of the United States or all the flags of the United Nations combine to make a world community. If there is time left, take the opportunity to write about how the group of flags represents your writing community, school, neighborhood, or city. Finish the day with a few more readings from journals. The families can take their flags home with them, but it might be more important to display them prominently, at least until your project comes to its end.

In this next sample meeting, you are going to ask the families whether they want to bring food to share at the next meeting. Invite them to bring food or dishes that in some way represent their families. Maybe these will be favorite snacks such as popcorn or chips with sour cream and onion dip, or they might be traditional family recipes like deviled eggs or macaroni and cheese.

Week Three

- Sign-in
- Food
- Journal writing about food
- Sharing journal writing
- Family stories, brainstorming, and writing
- Reading aloud

This week assumes that you've asked families to bring food. All of the Family Scribe Groups I have heard from had potlucks and recipe sharing at some time during their project. Families enjoy sharing food both because eating delicious food and writing seem to go together so well and because they learn aspects of other families' lives while talking and writing about the various dishes everyone brings. Begin with a couple of prompts:

> *What does the food you chose to bring today say about your family?*
> *What special memories do you associate with food, family dinners, or cooking?*

While families arrive, get settled, and devour their plates of food, they can write in their journals. When the right time comes, go around the room, letting anyone who wants to share read aloud what he or she has written. Or you might group families together and ask them to share their writings in small groups. Then each group can nominate one or two members to read their pieces for the entire class.

Now that bellies are full and stories have been told, it is time for the day's main activity, which is the remembering and telling of family stories. In keeping with the theme of "Family Matters," explain that everyone will write a poem or story about an incident, some memory that stands out as being important to their family.

I recommend beginning by demonstrating some sort of brainstorming technique. You might have an idea web already completed about your own family memories that you can show. Maybe your web will have branches with themes such as family vacations, rules at home, holiday traditions, or helping others. Or you might have a long list of memories that you can read aloud, sharing small bits of information about some of the memories as you go along.

Once everyone has the idea, let the group members work in their journals, creating their own brainstorms. Those who finish early can grab another plate or begin writing. When it looks like the brainstorms are for the most part finished, stop everyone for a few minutes to share, maybe within their own family groups or perhaps with the entire group.

At this point, I would have a story or poem already written about an important memory from my own brainstorm that I could read. Then it is the families' turn to see what they can create out of the memories they have pulled from their family life.

If you used small groups earlier in the class when sharing food memories, you might again arrange families in groups to share their memory writing. Or you can simply let anyone who wants to read take turns reading for the class. I think it is pretty certain that the various poems and stories this activity inspires will lead to conversations and discussions about similar experiences, so be prepared to let the families respond to one another, either while taking turns sharing or at the end of class.

For the next class, ask families to bring food a second time. It has been my experience, as well as that of other project facilitators, that the first potluck is enough of a success to motivate everyone to want to bring food for following class sessions.

Week Four

- Sign-in
- Family roles brainstorm and prompt
- Family sculptures
- Writing about family sculptures

Begin with a discussion of the roles each person plays at home. What are the activities they most engage in? How do they interact with each other? What do they do that plays a part in family life? After the discussion, it is time to introduce the idea of family sculptures.

Family sculptures are a way of letting each family act out their roles. How will they do this? Each family group needs to decide how they can arrange and pose their family to show how the various members act when together. Then they will strike poses that visually represent their roles. For instance, a mother may feel that her main role is working to earn money for her three children to live comfortably. She may stand with her debit card in hand and act out receiving and spending money. One daughter may be the chief caretaker for her younger siblings, so she might stand with her hands on her hips, looking primarily at them. A younger brother might have the important job of setting the table for dinner every night, so he might go through the motions of laying out plates, glasses, and silverware.

After each family has worked out their living sculptures, it is time to perform for the rest of the group. Let each family act out their roles, giving other families the chance to guess what they are doing and why those parts are important to the family as a whole.

Once all the performances have ended, it is time to write. The writings can take different approaches. A father could write about how he feels about his role, or he might write about how the roles of his wife and children support or complement his part. A child might write about how he or she appreciates the roles played by a mother or siblings. The writing may be paragraphs, letters, poems, or word lists. Let each person find the best way to analyze and respond to the experience. It's possible that some might want to write about another family's performance or the effect that the exercise has had on them.

It might be an interesting activity to ask all of the families to simultaneously perform their sculptures. This chaotic group performance could lead to a discussion of community and the different ways in which families combine to create a neighborhood or community.

As a final activity, ask each person to list several things they could do, roles that they could fulfill, in the coming week or weeks before your next meeting. Ask them to think of acts that they do not usually fulfill. For example, a mother might include in her list reading a story to her youngest daughter after dinner. An oldest son could include the idea of walking his younger brother home from school. Challenge everyone to pick one idea from his or her lists to act out in real life before the next meeting. Let them know that they will report on what they decided to do, and invite them to write about how they felt or how the action affected other members of the family.

Week Five

- Sign-in
- Brief review of previous weeks
- Role challenge follow-up
- Important dates and days
- Calendar making

Now that you are in the last week, it is time to review everything that you have done. This would be a good time to give family members the chance to comment on the project or to find out what activities they enjoyed most. I can envision inviting everyone to respond to a journal prompt on the project during the time between when they arrive and class officially begins. For example, everyone will have something to write about if given the question "How did you grow as a result of the group?" as a prompt.

Next, each family will work together to create a list of dates and days that they find important. This might take the form of an idea web, or it might just be a long list of birthdays, holidays, anniversaries, church meeting days, or any other days of the year that stand out in their lives.

Take a few minutes to let the families share their brainstorms, then challenge them to pick several from their lists to write about. Whatever they choose, no two members of any family should write about the same day. There may be enough time for some to finish two or more short writings.

Take time to read aloud and respond. Then introduce the group's final project, which is to create a family calendar.

Culminating Project

Calendar making as a culminating project provides a way for Family Scribe Groups to publish their work. Calendars also require group members to collaborate on design and contents. Finally, each calendar will become a lasting reminder of the Scribe Group and the impact it had on members' lives.

I hope that you have access to a computer lab. In case you do not, I include some suggestions for how to make the calendars without access to multiple computers at the end of this section of the chapter.

In the lab, make sure there are a scanner and a printer. Also, bring along a digital camera to take family and group photos. Families will use the scanner to capture their family flags from Week Two and to scan any other photos or artifacts they might want to include among their calendar pages. They can type up final copies of any of their writings from the project on the computer and then spend the rest of the time fitting the various scanned objects and writings on the calendar pages.

If you are creating standard wall calendars with twelve pages, place the writing and photos on the backs of the months so that, as the calendar is turned, a new writing or picture comes on display. You can bind the calendars like books, with several pages between each calendar page. As a variation, it would be possible to create one anthology containing contributions from all of the families along with the calendar pages.

If you do not have access to a computer lab, bring blank pages and calendar pages to class for the families to fill in by hand. They can attach their writings and pictures to the blank pages, marking important dates. Each calendar can be bound, perhaps with yarn or string. It is possible that this handmade approach might even be preferable if you are working with lots of younger children or if your families are not very computer-savvy.

Frequently Asked Questions

Over the past several years, I have led workshops or presented at writing and reading conferences around the country and at National Writing Project sites. At every event, audiences ask a common set of questions. I base my responses to the questions that follow on my work with the Fremont Family Writing Project's Scribe Group. They also touch on insights I have gained from other Family Scribe Groups in Las Vegas and around the country.

How should I select families for participation in a Family Scribe Project?

Most elementary teachers have parent conferences. As a middle-school teacher, I am responsible for a yearly open house night when parents visit my classroom. Both of these situations are excellent opportunities for first mentioning Scribe Groups to parents. High-school teachers tell me that their open houses also work as a good opening for contacting families.

On open house night, my co-facilitators and I usually spend a few minutes after talking about our regular school-day classes to bring up the Family Scribe Group. We have sign-up sheets ready to collect the names of families who want to know more about our project. And we have anthologies and other artifacts, such as our CD, for families to look at.

It has been my experience that families who show up for Open House are also families who are likely to follow through on the commitment it takes to be productive members of a semester- or year-long Family Scribe Group. They have already shown me that they are willing to put forth a minimum amount of involvement in their children's educations by showing up at school for Open House. Keep in mind that you want your project to succeed—you will want to work with families who are going to show up for your Scribe Group.

I also think that all teachers will identify students in their classes who have an enthusiasm and aptitude for writing that goes beyond typical participation. I always pick out a handful of these students and contact their families. Just as with the parents who attend Open House night, I find that the parents of kids who love to write are more likely to follow through with an entire project. Really, it only makes sense that their children's enthusiasm for writing would inspire them to become excited about family writing.

I do not want to give the impression that I think Family Scribe Groups are only for successful students or "ideal" families, if there are such families. But these ways of selecting participants, especially for first-year projects, help to guarantee success. Forcing writing on families that do not want to be at school is only going to lead to frustration and varying degrees of failure. Building and expanding upon successful beginnings is important, not only for a project's facilitators but for its families as well. After all, the purpose of a Family Scribe Group is not to forcibly convert non-writers into authors, but rather, to create a situation that encourages writers to discover themselves.

Here in Las Vegas, Family Scribe Groups have twice been hosted by churches. In those situations, the facilitators, who were members of the congregations, made the projects open to all families of the churches. We also have offered a Family Scribe Group in Las Vegas through a local parks and recreation department, which listed the project alongside other classes in their catalog. If you are not in a school setting but want to facilitate a project, working with your local parks and recreation department might be a way to attract interested families.

How big should my project be?

Of the many Scribe Groups I have visited or been in contact with over the past few years, most began small. It seems that most in their first year involve four to seven families. That may not seem like many participants, but consider that a single family might include up to five or six members. A group with seven families can easily amount to more than 25 people in the room. If there is one constant cry among classroom teachers, it is to keep class size to a minimum. For Family Scribe Groups, particularly first-year projects, small is fine. I have talked to teachers who were worried because they only had twelve or thirteen people in their projects. To me, this situation is not problematic: small groups develop a strong sense of community and bond closely.

It is likely that first-year projects will grow in size from their first meeting to their last. And it is almost certain that a project will leap in size from its first year to its second year. Why? While new families are joining, families from the first year will want to remain involved.

I have observed that when a Family Scribe Group consistently has more than 35 or 40 family members showing up to write, it is easy for the project to lose meaningful interactions between families and for participants to keep distance between their families and others. Facilitators of large Family Scribe Groups need to develop activities that bring individual families into direct, purposeful interactions with one another. Also, facilitators of large groups might want to lead activities that break the large group into two or more smaller groups.

Can I facilitate a Family Scribe Group by myself?

Facilitating a Family Scribe Group is energizing, but it can also drain you with its various demands. Unless a project is especially large, with more than perhaps fifty participants, two facilitators can handle the work. If the group is even larger, you probably will want to find some way to split the group into two or more groups and involve a third or fourth facilitator.

There are many small things to take care of before you meet, such as gathering supplies, setting up the room, and putting together refreshments. There are also lots of decisions to make during a project, and it is always good to have someone with whom you can share ideas and develop plans. I have led a Family Scribe Group by myself but found that I was not as happy with the way the project went as when I have co-facilitated with others. I really missed sharing the experience with one of my peers.

Including individual families more and more in the planning process for our activities and writings has been a personal goal. Eventually, I would like to see families up in front of the group leading everyone through a complete lesson. The Fremont Family Scribe Group is actively working towards that goal. Now that we have families who have participated in the project for two or more years, I feel comfortable asking them to take on additional leadership and responsibilities. They understand our project and have seen what sorts of activities work best. And they bring unique perspectives as family members and non-school teachers that I, as a teacher/facilitator, do not possess. I hope that, through their increased involvement in planning and leading class, our Family Scribe Group continues to evolve and grow.

How do you fund your Family Scribe Group?

The Fremont Family Scribe Group has a number of varied sources for support. This range of financial support is important to us because it demonstrates community involvement with our project and makes us less dependent upon any individual source.

First, we have worked closely with the Southern Nevada Writing Project, the local National Writing Project site. The Southern Nevada Writing Project has helped our Family Writing Project, as well as many others in the Las Vegas area, with teacher stipends, materials, and other needs. Every state in the nation has local sites of the National Writing Project. If you are not already familiar with the National Writing Project, look online at www.nwp.org for information about the site nearest you. If you are a Teacher Consultant within the National Writing Project (a teacher who has completed a National Writing Project writing institute), go to your local site director to see if there is funding available to support your Family Scribe Group.

Another source for funding may be your city or community. The City of Las Vegas has awarded our project four different $1,000 neighborhood involvement grants. Check with your local government to see if money is available for community-based projects. We have also worked with a City of Las Vegas community park, Baker Park. The park houses Baker Community School, which is a part of the city's parks and recreation department. An important mission of the school is to provide classes and other services to the community around the park. It may be that your own local parks and recreation department has a similar mission and would be willing to help financially, with supplies, or by providing a place to meet.

If you are teaching in a school it is very likely that pressure is on teachers to work with families. Our own school, John C. Fremont Middle School, has been extremely helpful with providing basic supplies such as journals, pens, pencils, small door prizes for the children, and snacks. Explore the possibility that your school has access to grant money, such as Title I funds or 21st Century grants. Both of these have become steady sources of support for Family Scribe Groups in Las Vegas. Explore the possibility of obtaining local or state grants relating to literacy—one Las Vegas Family Writing Project in 2004 literally had problems finding ways to spend all of the funds they received as part of a very large literacy grant.

I do, however, have one concern about funding: I think it is extremely important that Family Scribe Groups remain as autonomous as possible. A project should belong to the families, not to a school district, community center, city, or other organization. Be concerned with surrendering ownership of the project as a consequence of accepting funding. If you are alert and communicate well with your funding sources about the purposes of your project, however, you should not have any problems.

When and where should my Family Scribe Group meet?

There is no standard answer to this question. In fact, it seems that almost every Family Scribe Group we hear from has a different day of the week and different time for meeting. The Fremont Family Scribe Group has always met on Saturday mornings or afternoons at our host school. Our families have said that they like to meet on Saturdays because they have too many other commitments during the week, including homework. Many elementary-school Family Scribe Groups meet right after school one or two days a week for only an hour. Parents are already coming to school to pick up their children, so it is a good time for them to spend a little extra time at school.

In Las Vegas, there are Family Scribe Groups that meet twice a week after school for an hour, once a week after school for two hours, once a month for three hours, and every other weekend. But projects do not have to meet at schools. One project has told us that they meet at the homes of project members. Other Las Vegas projects have met at churches and a local parks and recreation facility. The key, I think, is to be flexible and determine what will work best for yourself and your families.

I think that a project needs at least two hours in order to get meaningful work accomplished. The only project I know of that meets for only one hour meets on consecutive days during the week—that works for them. Find what works for you and your families.

What time of the year works best for Family Scribe Groups?

Although the Fremont Family Scribe Group originally met in the spring semester, we have also met in the fall. In fact, now our project runs throughout the school year. The main advantage for a fall Scribe Group is that the relationships that were forged between me as a teacher and my students and their families established friendships that lasted all year. My students get to work with me on fun and meaningful writing and they get to share that experience with their families. I believe that my students see me in a new light, one that differs from the classroom setting. They see that I really care about them, and they also see me more as a person than simply as a teacher.

When our project begins in the fall, I also have the chance to get to know parents rather than just meeting them briefly at Open House or in a parent conference. The group also gives parents a chance to know and work with their children's teachers. Of course, by starting early in the school year, we all have the chance to develop a strong sense of community and belonging. For families, the school becomes a community meeting place where they feel comfortable to talk, discuss, and write about their lives. This is especially true when our project continues through the spring until the end of the school year.

What should I do about families that do not speak English?

Language often becomes one of the defining characteristics of Family Scribe Groups. Take into account your community's diversity, and be certain that your project represents the population you serve. If you do not speak a language or languages used by family members, see if you can find someone to co-facilitate the project who does. When possible, translate notes and invitations that you send home into the languages families speak. Welcome writers to write in their mother tongues during the project. The point of a Family Scribe Group is to create opportunities for writing, not to specifically teach English as a second language.

With all of that said, you may find that speakers of languages other than English will want to take advantage of this rare chance for them to write in English. Quite a few times I have watched Spanish-speaking mothers and fathers in Family Scribe Groups work hard to craft poems or paragraphs in English and then read their words aloud minutes after finishing.

I suppose my best answer is to value and appreciate a family's languages and to find opportunities to let them write in the ways most comfortable or appropriate for them.

How do you keep families involved?

As much as I hope that families will love writing and find motivation purely from the rewards they find each time they set pencil to paper, I know that there are many other factors coming into play each time we invite families to join our Family Scribe Group.

The project competes with soccer practice, weekend shopping, family trips, visits by relatives, and myriad other interests and commitments. If families are going to dedicate a portion of their busy lives to coming to school on weekends or in the afternoon or evening, we want them to know that we appreciate their involvement. I do that by staying in constant touch during our project.

A month or more before we begin, we send home invitation letters and a second sign-up sheet. Then, as the date for our first meeting approaches, we mail home store-bought invitations, the same kind that people use as party invitations. The week of our first class, we make calls home to touch base and answer any questions.

I hope that each family's experience at the first project meeting will be strong enough to draw them back for more. Just in case it isn't, we always send thank-you notes in the mail and another letter home with students with a word of thanks and information about our next meeting. Throughout each of our projects, we try to maintain this constant contact with families at home. Hopefully, when they look at the calendar to make plans, they will see that the Family Scribe Group already has a place in their schedules.

Do you grade family writings? Do you work specifically on the mechanics or conventions in their writings?

There is no reason to grade the writings families create because our Scribe Groups are not competitive. Generally, we do not work on mechanics or conventions either. I can see how it might benefit some of the writers to look at how to improve those aspects of their writings, but our main concern has always been with expression. I want family writers to put their thoughts and beliefs into writing without feeling held back by periods, capitals, and prepositions.

Rather than spending more of our time together editing or revising, it has been helpful to write about our project and discuss how it affects members' lives. Overwhelmingly, Family Scribe Group members feel liberated and empowered by the opportunity to write. Self-perception surveys are fun, too. Writers like to look at their growth in how they feel about themselves as writers.

We do publish our works, however, both in print anthologies and on the Internet at our website. Several Las Vegas Family Scribe Groups use their school's computer labs for a few hours at the end of their project to revise and edit finished drafts of pieces written earlier during their projects. At those sessions, facilitators help with editing and revising but usually only when asked. More often than not, family members decide themselves how they want to finish the pieces.

In class, when we are writing, we facilitators point out strong elements of writing craft, such as word choice. We emphasize these qualities in our examples and applaud writers when they craft strong images in their writing. As a consequence, we find that many of our Scribes turn out strong and vivid writing.

What is the best way to keep track of all the writing families create from week to week?

One thing for certain is that your group is going to generate a lot of writing during the weeks you write together. It is truly a challenge to hold on to all of that writing. In the early days of the Fremont Family Scribe Group, we gave complimentary writing journals to all of our members for each meeting. This seemed like a great idea, but it led to problems. Invariably, journals were lost. Members also forgot to bring them to class. When it came time to create our anthologies or work on the website, many pieces of writing were lost.

We still pass out journals at our first meeting, but those are for the writers to use at home for whatever purposes they find. In class, we use Family Scribe binders to hang onto all the poems, lists, essays, and other writings that we generate. Each family has a binder with their name on it. In each folder is plenty of notebook paper. As members finish each piece, they store them in their families' binders. We, the facilitators, then keep the folders at school until our next meeting, when we pull them out and give them back to our writers.

At the end of each project, families usually keep the binders. If there are pieces of writing that we facilitators want to keep track of, we make photocopies. This approach sits well with the families because it frees them from the burden of having to show up each week with their journals. For facilitators, it ensures that work is not lost and is available for later use.

What should I do about members who do not want to write?

Respect reluctant writers. Do not make fun of them or put them down for not putting pen to paper from the start. Rather, find ways to encourage them that build upon their lives and knowledge base. Hesitant writers will almost always be adult family members. They may not have expected that they were going to write with their children, or they may have had bad writing experiences before ever joining your group.

I have found that reluctant writers are either swept up in the writing climate of Family Scribe Groups or they stop attending. Every now and then, an adult drops out of the group and is replaced by another family member. Usually, though, that is not the case. Nine times out of ten, the person who at first does not want to write later becomes one of the most enthusiastic writers in the group, someone everyone looks forward to hearing read aloud.

Besides writing skills, what skills do children gain from participation in a Family Scribe Group?

Children in Family Scribe Groups often undergo genuine personality transformations. Parents consistently comment on the growth and development they see in their children as a consequence of their participation. Some children find ways of talking about deeply personal feelings and thoughts with their families. They develop an openness and sincerity that their parents before had not seen.

Family Scribe Groups also bring out leadership skills in children. In Scribe Groups, children work with others, including adults. Often, such as in the planning of an anthology or design of a garden, it is the children who take the lead. In the Fremont Family Scribe Group, our young members have made grant presentations to the City of Las Vegas and have worked with city personnel to order and receive materials for our work. While these experiences are at first intimidating to the students, they quickly come to believe in themselves and their ideas.

Shyness disappears in many students. In Scribe Groups they meet new people with whom they share strong experiences. The very act of putting their thoughts on paper and then standing up to read them aloud in a room full of fellow writers calls upon them to summon up courage and bravery that many people never develop.

Perhaps the most obvious area of growth for many of the children is their development of a strong sense of community. In a Family Scribe Group, children find that they can become important contributors. They listen and learn from others and offer their own ideas. Many groups focus on themes that naturally lend themselves to concern for community. The students learn that they are members of communities. This knowledge shows up in their writing and is reflected in culminating activities such as gardens, murals, or other community-minded projects.

What surprises do parents encounter in Family Scribe Groups?

Parents often do not understand what they are getting into when they show up at that first Family Scribe Group class session. Although we take pains to explain the concepts surrounding our project at Open House nights, in letters home and in phone calls, many parents arrive for the first meeting not realizing that they are going to write alongside their kids. Quite often, they come with the idea that they are going to sit back and watch—or worse, wait outside in the car!

I do not think they are to blame for this set of expectations, or lack thereof. Most parents will send their children through twelve years of school without ever once being invited to join in, to learn alongside their children, and to model learning themselves. How could they arrive uninitiated and know that during the project they will work through the same writing processes that their children do every day in school? How could they predict that in the process they will learn about themselves as well as their children? I imagine that some parents recall their own years at school and are expecting some sort of grammar class with preposition worksheets and subject-verb exercises.

Parents, grandparents, older siblings, and other relatives inevitably come away from their time at the Family Scribe Group with changed perspectives. Many discover author's voices within themselves that they had never expected to uncover. Had they not come to the Scribe Group, they might never have seen themselves as writers. There are always some who vow to continue with journals and family writing at home. From their experiences with writing, they find that they now have ways of working with memories, feelings, and ideas that before did not have any outlets.

Most importantly, the ways in which parents understand their children change during Family Scribe Groups. Children become very grown-up in their parents' eyes. Parents watch and listen as their children discuss and write about issues as equals in a close-knit community.

A mother in a Las Vegas Family Scribe Group put it this way: "Sometimes, as the parent of a teenaged daughter, I find myself cringing at what might come out of her mouth at home. She's always reacting to something we do or say. But here, I see her thinking through her ideas and sharing them in a very adult way. This project is showing me another side of my daughter—a side that has always been there, maybe. I just didn't have any way to see it until now."

Many parents new to Family Scribe Groups never consider that such a change in the way they think about their children will come about through participation in a writing workshop.

How do you put together a print anthology?

Anthologies are one of the most important lasting artifacts of Family Scribe Groups. Families assemble different types of writing, photographs, and artwork created during their projects. For these reasons, anthologies have always been a staple of Family Scribe Groups.

As a facilitator, it is best to involve families in the process of making the anthology. Rather than spending time alone typing up pieces and assembling the book, I now invite the families into our school's computer lab for an afternoon of word processing. Together, we select the works to be included in our anthology, and we edit and revise. This process not only involves the families directly in the production of the book but also saves me hours—days, even—of solitary work. We add writings to our website in the same way.

Anthologies are often the most expensive undertaking of Scribe Groups. It can easily cost several hundred dollars to produce a sharp-looking anthology with a color cover, several pages of color photos, and binding that will last. Keep this fact in mind when writing up your budget or seeking grant money. Explore other ways to cut corners on costs, such as approaching your school or another community-oriented group with the hopes of involving them in production. You can bind your anthology yourself at school or approach your school district or a local church to make color copies for your group at a discount.

In Their Own Words: Facilitators Speak

W hile it has been only a few years since the first Family Scribe Group began as part of the larger Fremont Family Writing Project at John C. Fremont Middle School in Las Vegas, the spread of groups to sites in Las Vegas and other cities around the country has been phenomenal. It seems that each time I speak on Scribe Groups at a conference or gathering of teachers, someone in the room goes to start his or her own project.

Twice, once in the fall of 2003 and again in the summer of 2004, I sat down with facilitators in Las Vegas. Some were entirely new to Family Scribe Groups; their projects were still in the planning stages. Others had facilitated groups for a year or more at schools and churches in Las Vegas. Heading into our two meetings, I had several questions that I was curious to hear answered.

I wanted to know why these people had decided to establish Family Scribe Groups. What about the groups had so captured their imaginations that they felt compelled to facilitate groups of their own? I also was curious to find out from those who had already facilitated a Scribe Group what had worked for them and the families. Similarly, I wanted to know what difficulties they had encountered and what unexpected outcomes developed throughout the course of their projects. Finally, I wondered if the facilitators, all of whom were also teachers at the same Las Vegas schools where they held their Scribe Group meetings, could identify ways in which the experience has affected their classroom teaching.

Why start a Family Scribe Group?

Facilitators have a variety of explanations for why they have decided to work with families. Facilitator Tom Frasier saw that the Family Scribe Group fills a void that schools do not address. He felt that, even before beginning to work with families, it was "clear that the Scribe Group can accomplish things for our students, our community, and our teachers that the school district can't accomplish, no matter how much they want to." The Scribe Group setting, with its focus on community and on issues that matter to families, as well as on direct family involvement, generates new perspectives that just cannot be explored or created in the school-day classroom. For Tom, leading a Scribe Group also gave him "some of the autonomy some of us are always looking for" as teachers. In other words, leading a Family Scribe Group enabled him to break free from issues such as curriculum demands, subject area benchmarks, and district mandates to create, with families, new opportunities in education.

Marie Kinghorn, who facilitated a Family Scribe Group at a Las Vegas middle school, brought another perspective to the discussion when she said, "My biggest draw, I think, to the program when I first heard about it was it dealt with families." For Marie, working with the families of her students opened new doors that she believed would lead to great places: "I'm an optimist, I'm an idealist, and I think little things can change the world. I think if we can build a stronger sense of family, even just by starting with a little program in our schools, we can make things better." Marie's optimism and belief in the potential of Scribe Groups to effect change in the world is an idea that families also often express.

As Julie Kofford, a mother in the Fremont Family Scribe Group wrote in class one day, "This project has taught us that one small voice, our small voice, can and does change the world around us for the better. We've come together for the betterment of our own lives, for the betterment of each other, for the betterment of those around us that belong to this community. And most of all, for the betterment of our children who will one day carry on that small voice to those who will come after us." As Julie expresses so well, families in Scribe Groups recognize that they are creating ripples of change and creativity with real effects for themselves and others.

Another Las Vegas facilitator, Elizabeth Campbell, emphasized ways in which the Scribe Group experience influences parents by involving them at school and, in the process, directly with their children's learning. She said that, before beginning her project, "One of the roadblocks I kept running into as a teacher was that my kids were having troubles and my kids' parents weren't particularly educated. They lacked the resources to help the kids at home." At the same time, she emphasized, "They were very good parents and very loving and supportive parents." For her, the Scribe Group was a way to "bring those parents into the school and give them the resources, or maybe to give them ways to help their kids."

The Scribe Group experience is a powerful link between school and home that just does not exist in the standard school setting. As Shaunene Edwards, a mother in the Fremont Family Writing Project, put it, "One of the most important benefits of this project for me as a mom is that I'm getting to know my children better through their writing. After we leave each project meeting, we have a discussion about our writing, and anytime parents and their children can communicate, it is a great thing. The Fremont Family Scribe Group builds a great bridge from the school to the community." Shaunene clearly recognized that Scribe Groups bring relevance to writing, making it a starting point for communication within families and making a meaningful connection between what might normally be thought of as just schoolwork with families' lives.

Emma Perkins, who has facilitated Family Scribe Groups at both schools and churches in Las Vegas, hit upon an idea similar to Elizabeth's when she pointed out that as teachers, "We went to school for four years to learn how to do what we're doing." But often teachers "expect our parents, who might not have a high-school education, to do the same things" that we achieve in the classroom.

Teachers, without realizing it, often expect parents to have the pedagogical backgrounds of teachers with years of training, an assumption both unfair and unrealistic. For Emma, the Scribe Group is an opportunity to "pull parents in and show them education in a fun light." It is also a way to let the parents "show how they really care, to let them interact with their children and teachers, and show that they care about solving these roadblocks that they're having." Emma added that, "as a teacher, it's a sigh of relief" to see parents actively involved, not only working with their kids but also growing as writers and becoming members of the school community.

Tracy Rush, who has led Family Scribe Groups at two school sites in Las Vegas, said she facilitates because it is a chance for her to open her heart to her students and their families: "They filled it to overflowing by their enthusiasm, effort, and gratitude. Our voices were lifted up along with our spirits." Her thoughts express that elusive emotional aspect of Family Scribe Groups, the crucial element of the projects that is so hard to measure and quantify. But this important emotional component does exist and is so often the magic element that families and facilitators alike point to as the strongest reason they have for wanting to belong to Scribe Groups.

What worked in your Family Scribe Group?

When asked what had worked, facilitators provided answers that had more to do with overall outcomes than with specific activities. One big success, facilitators felt, was the autonomy their projects gave them as teachers and the resulting confidence they developed as professionals. Elizabeth Campbell, in her first year as a facilitator, stuck very closely to the activities shared in **Chapters 3 through 7** of this book, an approach that she said was "meaningful" and "positive" for her and her families. She added that the first year's success gave her confidence and a sense of creativity that carried over to her second year, when she designed an entirely new project called "How Does Your Garden Grow?" With this theme, the Scribe Group explored the "positive and negative influences in families' lives and their hopes and aspirations for the future." For Elizabeth, the answer to the question of what worked was that she grew as a teacher as a result of her experiences writing with families.

Emma Perkins chimed in with similar ideas when she said that facilitating gave her "as a professional a chance to teach writing for the pure joy of it without having to worry about grading." As an educator, she felt freed up to focus on what really mattered. She also found it "energizing to see the excitement on the faces of participants as we did writing prompts. They were almost like racehorses straining to get out of the gate to race and to write." Emma and her families did the balloon prompt activity outlined in **Chapter 5** of this book, which she says "was good for the kids because it got them moving, and when we popped the balloons and had prompts to write with, they were just ready to write." When students and families bring this level of excitement to writing, it becomes obvious that writing for the sake of communication and expression, rather than for the sake of grades, is a powerful aspect of Scribe Groups that works. Writing, for families, is a real and potent activity.

Tracy Rush found several things that worked in the three Family Scribe Groups she led at two different schools, one at a high school and two at a middle school. She said that the Scribe Groups she has facilitated have had a hand in "improving the dynamics of students, teachers, and families working together." They also provided "a sense of community and a greater understanding of each individual's role in the community."

A somewhat unexpected success of her project was that it "served as a key to opening doors among faculty members who were curious about writing." Her colleagues were impressed by families and teachers who were willing to sacrifice their time and come together on weekends to engage in learning and community service activities. The project's effect was felt beyond her and her families. The entire school community took notice of what she and the families accomplished, and this outcome was an important success for Tracy because it added validation to the work her groups had undertaken.

How has facilitating a Family Scribe Group influenced your classroom teaching?

Facilitators of Scribe Groups who are teachers notice changes when they return to the classroom. Kids from their projects who are students in their classes see themselves as writers, a self-perception which makes them leaders in the classroom. Their enthusiastic leadership makes it easier for teachers to work with other, less experienced students. Teachers find that their experiences with families of students make them more understanding and open-minded when dealing with non-project students. They are more aware of family circumstances and students' lives away from school. The support that facilitators feel from parents translates into confidence for teachers in the classroom. They know that what they do has an impact, and they know that members of the school community recognize that impact and offer them support.

Marie Kinghorn said that she is now "more aware of the fact that outside influences have tremendous impact on how kids behave in class." She is more conscious of the image she projects to her students, she said, and she wonders, "What, if any, adults do they have to look up to outside of school? Do they have support and guidance?" This sort of empathy for students is something that many facilitators say they carry from their projects to their classrooms.

Marie also learned from writing with families how important a role talking plays in the writing process. In the Family Scribe Group, stories and discussions are important prewriting activities. In her classroom, Marie now makes "more of an effort to make talk a big part of my classroom writing process. My classes spend a lot of time talking about their lives, their interests, or whatever they feel the need to discuss." The change is good for both Marie and her students: "I have benefited from these talks as much as my students because I have gained their trust. They are more willing to open up and put more depth in their writing."

Tom Frasier, after working with Scribe Group families on so much writing about their lives and where they are from, brought an increased emphasis on place-based writing into his classroom. While parents in his project longed for places they had left, "The children, in turn, served to remind their parents that Las Vegas was home, that they themselves were a part of the fabric of a place. The parents, in stories of home, taught their children what was missing from this new world. The children challenged their parents to see what was present." In an urban setting like Las Vegas, where lives are very often transient, the Scribe Group's awareness of community and place works for parents as well as children and teaches both about the others' perspectives.

Tom made a fascinating observation about the sense of community that grows during Scribe Group meetings in an urban setting like Las Vegas: "In many ways, what the Scribe Group did was not new at all. It showed us what barn raising, threshing wheat, or quilting did to the diverse communities of America a century ago. It showed us that Las Vegas, if it is to build communities, will do so on the basis of affinity. People with widely different stories coming together to engage in a common pursuit, in this case writing." For him, writing is now a way to create community in the classroom by allowing students to express and share their lives.

Kim Sicurella expressed the influence of facilitating on her teaching as "bridging a gap between my students and me." Like all teachers, she recognized that "it is so easy for me to get caught up in the day-to-day routines of teaching that I sometimes forget to see my kids—I mean really see them for the individuals they are and what they have to offer as people, rather than as just part of my load of 150 students." Getting to know students on a more personal level during the Scribe Group, Kim said, has "taught me to do this during the week with all of my students. Each has something important to bring to class and to their writing. Everyone has a story to tell, a background to share." For Kim, getting to know her students in a setting outside the traditional classroom directly affects how she sees all of her students in her classroom. In turn, this change in her perspective affects how she teaches and how she relates to her students.

Like Marie, Kim stated that now she is more patient in class, more inclined to listen. "After sitting with a family to hear a story before they write, I realized how important it is that I sit and listen to my students' stories before they write, whether it's something they share from their journals or something that happened on the way to school that morning." Listening is not only for students. Marie's observation points to how important it is that teachers listen in order to learn from their students and to improve how they go about teaching. So much of what goes on in a Scribe Group centers around listening in order to develop understanding and generate ideas.

As you can see from the words of these facilitators, the experience of working with families and helping them to develop as writers has broad-reaching effects. Facilitators gain autonomy while helping to fill the gap that exists between school and home. They grow emotionally with their families and realize that they are able to help parents in new, useful ways. Schools feel the changes as the relationships with families and students take on new dimensions and classroom practices reflect changes in teachers who have led Family Scribe Groups.

I hope the ideas shared by these facilitators will stay with you as you embark on the journey of creating your own Scribe Group. The role of Family Scribe Group facilitator has the potential to become one of your most rewarding experiences as a writing teacher. Starting and leading a group requires some time commitment and the willingness to work with families in ways that go far beyond the typical after-school conference. Expect remarkable moments and highly thoughtful writing from your families, and you will not be disappointed. There really is no limit to how the experience will affect your life, both professionally and personally!

Templates

The following pages contain templates that you may want to use during your project.

Basic release. We usually distribute these with the binders at our first meeting and ask that families sign them and return them to us before leaving class. It is important for you to explain that, in most cases, nothing will be published before personally receiving permission from those involved. At our Fremont Family Scribe Group, families are usually directly involved in all of our publishing efforts, both in our anthologies and on our website. For using individual pieces for presentations to other teachers, however, we use the publicity release. If a family does not want to sign the release after having it explained, that is fine. However, make it clear to them that if they do not sign the release, they will not be able to participate in publishing efforts. Included are both an English and a Spanish version.

Family information sheet. Use this page to keep track of family members. Pass it out at your first meeting, then keep it on file. It will come in handy if you need to contact families at home and help you keep track of all the names in each family.

Fill-in-the-blank poems. Following the family information sheet are two templates to use for the fill-in-the-blank poem. The first is in English, the second in Spanish.

Homework assignments. One of these is for the photo-taking assignment ("Family Photographers!") and the other is for the mapmaking activity ("Communities We Know"). Both can be handed out at the end of Week Two, as described in **Chapter 4**. Or you can pass them out to families as your weekly schedule permits. Following each assignment sheet in English is a corresponding Spanish version.

Weekly plan. This will help you to organize your thoughts for each week of your project. It includes spaces for prompts, activities, materials, and homework.

Weekly self-evaluation. Facilitators use this for self-evaluating and documenting their work. It will help you to remember what you have done each week, evaluate your successes and failures, and plan for future projects.

Release
Family Scribe Group

Date: _____

Location: _____

I, _____, grant permission to the _____
Family Scribe Group to publish, either in print or electronically, copies of writing
that I and my children create during our Family Scribe Group. I also grant
permission for photographic images taken during the project to be published.

_____

name (please print)

_____

signature

Names of family members under 18 years of age:

_____

_____

_____

_____

_____

_____

Permiso de Autorización
Grupo de la Familia de Escritos

Fecha: _____

Localización: _____

Yo, _____ le doy permiso al Grupo de la Familia de
Escritos de _____ a publicar, ya sea por escrito o
electrónicamente, copias de escritos que mis hijos y yo creemos (realicemos)
durante nuestro Grupo de la Familia de Escritos. También doy permiso para que
se tomen fotografías durante el proyecto para que sean publicadas.

_____

nombre en letra imprenta

_____

firma

Nombres de miembros de familia menores de 18 años de edad:

_____

_____

_____

_____

_____

_____

Family Information Sheet
Página de Información de la Familia

Family name/Nombre de la familia: _____

Parents or Guardians/Padres o Guardiánes: _____

_____

Home phone/Teléfono del hogar: _____

Cell or emergency number/Teléfono celular o para emergencias: _____

Children's names/Nombres de los hijos:

_____

_____

_____

_____

_____

_____

_____

Fill-in-the-blank Poem

(Name): _____

From _____.

Who believes in _____,

And loves _____.

A person who would like to have _____,

Visit _____, and _____.

(Name): _____

A person who has fun when _____,

Whose funniest memory is the time when _____,

And whose most prized possession is his/her _____.

(Name): _____

A person who loves to eat _____,

Who is embarrassed when _____,

And who wants friends who _____.

(Name): _____

(Three adjectives describing yourself): _____, _____, and
_____.

Poema: Llene el espacio en blanco

(Nombre): _____

De _____,

quien cree en _____,

y ama a _____.

Una persona a quien le gustaría tener _____,

visitar _____ y _____.

(Nombre): _____

Una persona que se divierte cuando _____,

cuyo recuerdo más gracioso fue la vez que _____,

y cuya posesión más apreciada es su _____.

(Nombre): _____

Una persona a quien le encanta comer _____,

que tiene vergüenza cuando _____,

y que quiere amigos que _____.

(Nombre): _____

(Tres adjetivos que lo/la describan): _____, _____, and

_____.

Family Photographers!

You have your camera and note cards, but what are you going to take pictures of?

Good question.

With your cameras, snap shots of family things. You can take pictures of places your family goes. You might shoot photos of spots around your house. You can take snapshots of friends, grandparents, or little brothers and sisters.

Is there some favorite family restaurant or park? Do you have a favorite neighbor? Can you think of some place in town where something important for your family happened? Maybe you can take a photo of where you work or go to church?

Before our next meeting, have all your pictures taken. We'll collect your cameras and develop them for you. Then we'll give you back your photos, and we'll use them in class. You'll have the chance to share your favorite pictures with other families in class and write about them.

So have fun, and take some good pictures.

¡Fotógrafos de Familias!

Ustedes tienen sus cámaras y sus tarjetas con apuntes, pero ¿de qué van a tomar fotografías?

Buena pregunta.

Con sus cámaras, tomen fotos de cosas familiares. Saquen imágenes de los lugares a donde van sus familias. Pueden tomar fotos de diferentes partes de sus casas, y/o de sus amigos, abuelos, hermanitos o hermanitas.

¿Tienen algún restaurante o parque favorito? ¿Tienen algún vecino favorito? ¿Pueden pensar en algún lugar de la ciudad donde algo importante ocurrió con sus familias? Tal vez puedan tomar una foto de donde ustedes trabajan o donde van a la iglesia.

Antes de nuestra próxima reunión, asegúrense de tomar todas sus fotografías. Nosotros recogeremos sus cámaras y las desarrollaremos por ustedes. Luego les devolveremos sus fotografías y las usaremos en clase. Tendrán la oportunidad de compartir sus fotos favoritas con las otras familias de la clase y escribir sobre ellas.

¡Así que diviértanse y saquen buenas fotos!

Communities We Know

Think of where you live. Remember where you have lived. Can you draw those communities?

For this activity, you parents will draw what you remember of where you grew up. Try to create a map that shows some of the important places or landmarks. Was there a path home from school that you used to follow? Maybe there was a field where you used to play or a shopping center where you hung out. On a piece of graph paper, create any sort of map that you can, including as many memorable places as possible.

Kids, we want you to think about where you live now, where you have been growing up. You, too, will draw maps of those places. Your map might focus on your house or neighborhood, or it might be of the whole city. However you decide to draw your map, don't forget to include the places that you like, the places that you visit.

Parents and kids: when you finish your maps, write a short introduction that says something about the place. Include ideas such as where it is, how long you've lived there, and how you feel about the place. In class, we will show the maps and then read the pieces you've written. If we have time, we'll write more during class.

When drawing your maps, feel free to use any art supplies or map-drawing talents that you possess. Let those memories flow!

Comunidades que Conocemos

¿Piensan del lugar donde viven? ¿Se acuerdan de dónde vivían? ¿Pueden dibujar esas comunidades?

Para esta actividad sus padres van a dibujar el lugar donde ustedes recuerdan haber crecido. Traten de crear un mapa que muestre algunos lugares de importancia. ¿Había un camino en particular de la casa a la escuela que solían seguir? Tal vez había un campo donde jugaban o un centro comercial donde pasaban tiempo. En un papel de gráfica, dibujen cualquier tipo de mapa que puedan, e incluyan todos los lugares memorables posibles de los que se acuerden.

Niños, queremos que piensen de donde viven ahora, de donde están creciendo. Ustedes también van a dibujar mapas de esos lugares. Sus mapas pueden enfocarse en sus casas o en su vecindad, o pueden ser de toda la ciudad. De todas maneras, ustedes deciden el mapa que van a dibujar; no se olviden de incluir los lugares que les gustan y que visitan.

Padres y niños: cuando terminen sus mapas, escriban una pequeña introducción que diga algo del lugar. Incluyan ideas tales como dónde está, cuánto tiempo han vivido allí, y cómo se sienten sobre ese sitio. En clase vamos a mostrar los mapas y luego vamos a leer lo que han escrito. Si tenemos tiempo, escribiremos más durante la clase.

Cuando dibujen sus mapas pueden usar todos los suministros que quieran, y emplear todos los grandes talentos artísticos para dibujar mapas que posean. ¡Dejen brotar todas sus memorias!

Weekly Plan

Date: _____

Week number: _____

Theme for the week: _____

Opening prompt for families to write about while the group arrives. This should deal with the weekly theme: _____

_____

_____

Activity #1: _____

_____

_____

_____

Activity #2: _____

_____

_____

Activity #3: _____

_____

_____

Materials needed: _____

_____

_____

_____

Homework, if applicable: _____

_____

_____

Weekly Self-evaluation

Date: _____
Location: _____
Time: _____

Number of families involved: _____
Total number of participants: _____

Activities:

1.

2.

3.

4.

What worked best?

Any problems or difficulties?

How would you rate the meeting?